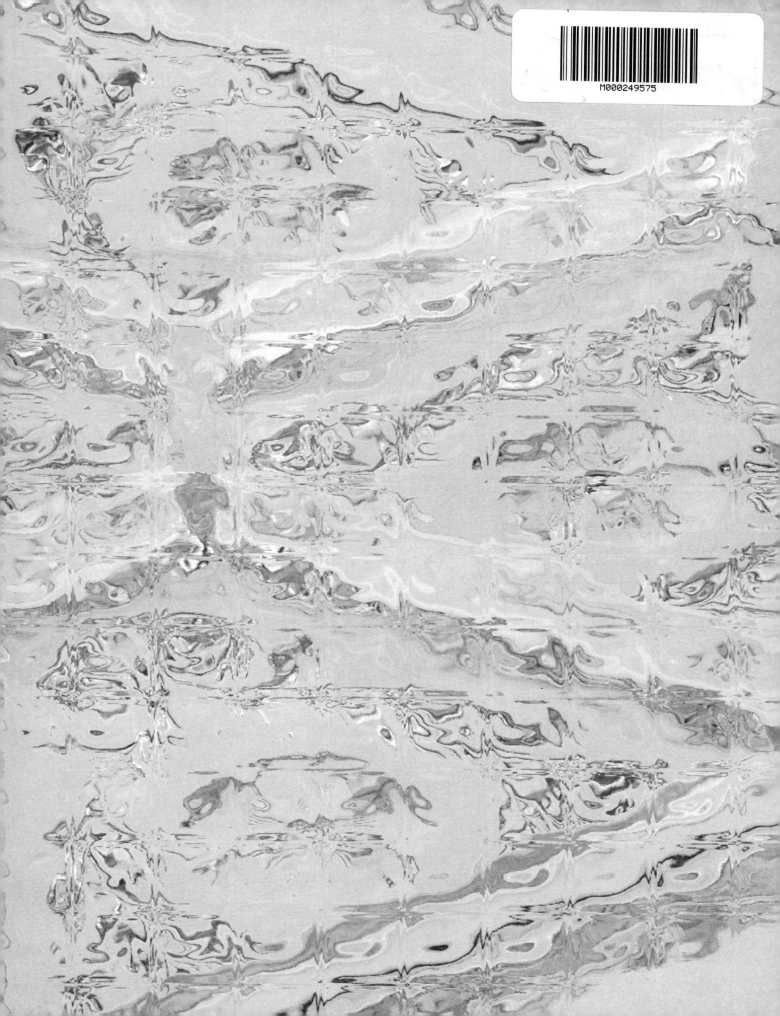

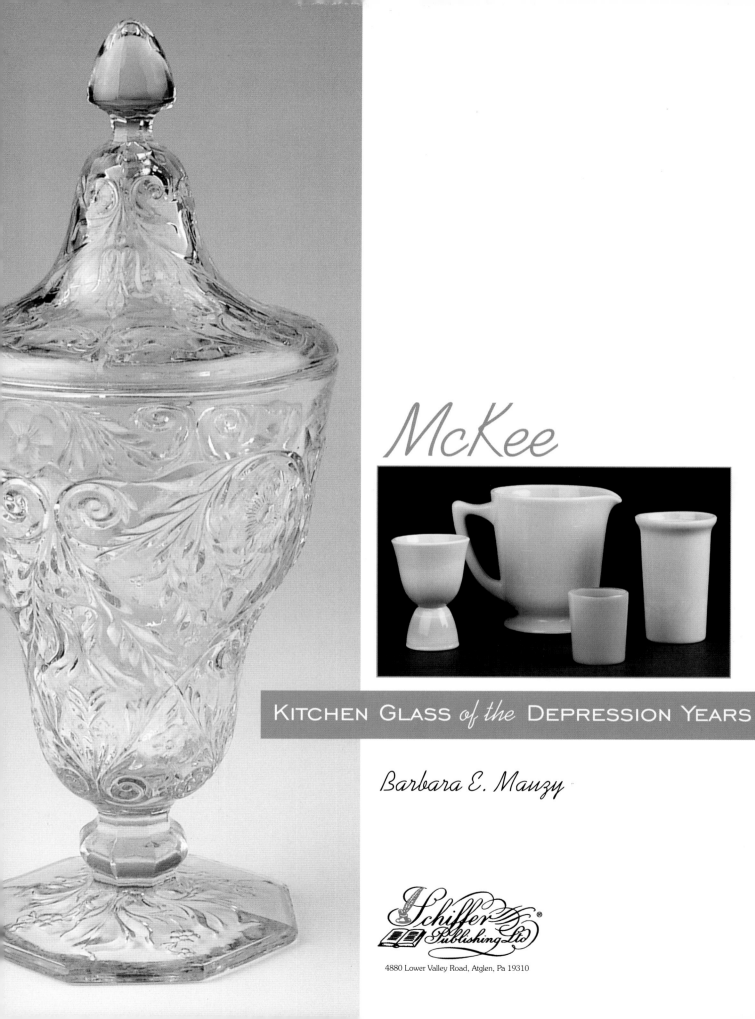

McKee

KITCHEN GLASS *of the* DEPRESSION YEARS

Barbara E. Mauzy

Schiffer
Publishing Ltd

4880 Lower Valley Road, Atglen, Pa 19310

Other Schiffer Books by Barbara Mauzy:
Peanut Butter Glasses, 2nd Edition
Bakelite in the Kitchen, 2nd Edition
The Complete Book of Kitchen Collecting, 2nd Printing
Sour Cream Glasses
Depression Era Kitchen Shakers
Gay and Gifty Pot Holders
PYREX The Unauthorized Collector's Guide, 4th Edition
Kitchen Treasures

Other books by Barbara and Jim Mauzy:
Mauzy's Kitchen Collectibles
Mauzy's Cake Plates
*Mauzy's Comprehensive Handbook of Depres
ion Glass Prices* (updated annually so contact the
Mauzys for a current edition)
Mauzy's Depression Glass, 5th Edition (updated every
other year so contact the Mauzys for a current edition)
Mauzy's Rare, Unusual, and Unique Depression Glass
(their newest title!)

Schiffer Books are available at special discounts for bulk purchases for sales promotions or premiums.
Special editions, including personalized covers, corporate imprints, and excerpts can be created in large
quantities for special needs. For more information contact the publisher:

Published by Schiffer Publishing Ltd.
4880 Lower Valley Road
Atglen, PA 19310
Phone: (610) 593-1777; Fax: (610) 593-2002
E-mail: Info@schifferbooks.com

For the largest selection of fine reference books on this and related subjects, please visit our
web site at **www.schifferbooks.com**
We are always looking for people to write books on new and related subjects. If you have an
idea for a book please contact us at the above address.

This book may be purchased from the publisher.
Include $5.00 for shipping.
Please try your bookstore first.
You may write for a free catalog.

In Europe, Schiffer books are distributed by
Bushwood Books
6 Marksbury Ave.
Kew Gardens
Surrey TW9 4JF England
Phone: 44 (0) 20 8392-8585; Fax: 44 (0) 20 8392-9876
E-mail: info@bushwoodbooks.co.uk
Website: www.bushwoodbooks.co.uk
Free postage in the U.K., Europe; air mail at cost.

Designed by RoS
Type set in Souvenir Lt BT

ISBN: 978-0-7643-3084-1
Printed in China

In memory of
Arnie Masoner
a collector, a dealer, a gentleman

Contents

ACKNOWLEDGMENTS   6

ABOUT THE VALUES   7

AN HISTORICAL OVERVIEW OF McKEE GLASS COMPANY   8

 Clarification of McKee Kitchen Glass Items   14

Part One: KITCHEN GLASS BY COLOR   20

 Black Kitchen Glass   21

  Plain or Undecorated

  Red Trim

 Blue Kitchen Glass   28

  Chalaine

  Cobalt

  Delphite

  Peacock

 Caramel Kitchen Glass   37

 Crystal Satinized or Frosted Kitchen Glass   38

 Fired-On Kitchen Glass   38

 French Ivory Kitchen Glass   39

  Plain or Undecorated

  Decorated Dots

  Diamonds

  Hand Painted Details

  Trimmed

 Green Kitchen Glass   65

  Satinized or Frosted

  Skokie Green (Jade-ite)

 Pink Kitchen Glass   84

 Seville Kitchen Glass   86

  Plain or Undecorated

  Decorated

  Seville with Black Glass

 White Kitchen Glass   95

  Plain or Undecorated

  Decorated

   Abraham Lincoln

   Advertising

   Bow Tie

   Diamonds

   Dots

   Flowers

   Miscellaneous

   Pennsylvania Dutch

   Ships

   Strawberries

  Trimmed

Part Two: DEPRESSION GLASS DINNERWARE   132

 Laurel   133

 Rock Crystal Flower   142

BIBLIOGRAPHY   156

INDEX   157

Acknowledgments

Whenever Jim and I create a book, we are reminded of how much there is to know regarding a subject and how knowledgeable and generous so many dealers and collectors are. I am indebted to these collectors and dealers who gave of their time, their expertise, and their glassware, which is featured throughout these pages. I hope their enthusiastic love of McKee glass passes from them to you via this book. My deepest thanks to each and every person who has contributed.

Denise Adams
Joanne Aldrich
Todd Baum and Jesse Speicher
Bob and Cindy Bentley
Ted Bradley
Clark Crawford
Tom Donlan
Ken and Terri Farmer
Bill and Patti Foti
John and Cindy Frank
Jewell Gowan
Connie and Bill Hartzell
Rick Hirte /
    Sparkle Plenty Glassware
Vic and Jean Laermans
Roger LeBlanc and Bryce Mansell
Walt and Kim Lemiski /
    Waltz Time Antiques

Arnie Masoner
Chuck Mauric
Randy Morey and Carol Miller
Wilma Morey
Larry Newton
Samantha Parish
Linda and Ron Peterson
Bill Quillen
Mike Rothenberger /
    Mike's Collectables
Staci and Jeff Shuck /
    Gray Goose Antiques
Faye and Robert Smith
Stephen Spaid
Jesse Speicher
Lynn and Faye Strait
Mike and Leegh Wyse
John and Marilyn Yallop

About the Values

The author has done everything possible to provide accurate prices by monitoring the Internet, auctions, trade papers, going to shows, and consulting with dealers and collectors. To this effort the author brings years of buying, selling, and collecting kitchen glassware, a personal favorite. Values vary immensely according to the condition of the piece, the location of the market, and the overall quality of the design and manufacture. Condition is always of paramount importance when assigning a value. The figures provided in this reference are for individual items that are in mint condition, but not packaged. When glassware retains original stickers or the original box the value is enhanced.

Prices in the Midwest differ from those in the West or East, and those at specialty shows such as Depression Glass shows will vary from those at general shows. In the current marketplace of volatile eBay end-of-auction results, it behooves us to acknowledge the same item can be offered at two different times and realize two very different values. Being at the right place, whether in person or online, at the right time can make all the difference.

All of these factors make it impossible to create an absolutely accurate values guide, but this books offers just that: a guide. Value shown reflect what one might realistically expect to pay but ultimately the seller and the buyer determine values as they agree upon a price, and we all want to make a purchase at the lowest amount possible but sell at the highest conceivable figure.

Neither the author nor the publisher are responsible for any outcomes resulting from this reference.

An Historical Overview of
McKee Glass Company

One American Contribution TO THE
American Home

The Beginning

McKee kitchen glass from the 1930s Depression era has roots decades old. The Phoenicians are credited with the discovery of glass in the first century AD. This synopsis will move forward to 1869 which bypasses over 250 years of the glass making industry in America.

The Early Years of McKee

McKee and Brothers Glass Works originated on the south side of Pittsburgh, Pennsylvania, in 1853, as producers of crystal glassware. "Crystal" refers to the clear color, not the mineral quartz crystal. McKee and Brothers was a successful enterprise that continued at this location until 1888. By then it had grown to occupy six acres of land with six furnaces and between five and six hundred employees/ The monthly payroll was $25,000. The pressed glass wares they produced were sold mostly in the United States, but twenty percent was exported to Europe. The high quality of McKee and Brothers handmade glassware rivaled cut glass and was in demand overseas.

The discovery of natural gas in Westmoreland County, southwest Pennsylvania, offered a necessary resource for glass manufacturing. Many glass companies relocated to this rural location where coke and coal were also plentiful for glass making.

In the spring of 1888, H. Sellers McKee, of the Western Land and Improvement Company of Philadelphia, and Pittsburgh investors Chambers and Brickell procured the farms of J. F. Thompson, Solomon Longhner, and J.F. Gilchrist, in Westmoreland County, for the establishment of a new glass factory almost thirty miles east of Pittsburgh. Workers employed at the factory and the goods and services they required quickly led to the development of a community. The town of Jeannette was born, named for H. Sellers McKee's wife. In April of 1888, home sites were plotted and construction of rows of brick homes commenced in June, on lots that initially sold for $400 apiece. Jeannette was the first community to be established in Westmoreland County, and by April 1889, four thousand individuals had relocated to this burgeoning town. The phenomenal growth was reflected in the increased value of land, as by June 1889 lots were purchased for $1200 each. At the turn of the twentieth century, this county had grown to be the sixth most populous county in Pennsylvania, and McKee and Brothers Glass Works had earned recognition for their production of milk (white) glass containers shaped as animals.

The National Glass Company acquired McKee and Brothers Glass Works in 1901, and the new name became McKee-Jeannette Glass Company. At its peak, National Glass Company consisted of nineteen factories; McKee-Jeannette was considered one of the best factories in the conglomerate. National Glass Company fell victim to discord among the directors, many of whom departed to develop competing businesses.

Also in 1901, the first "tec" patterns were introduced by McKee-Jeannette. "Tec" refers to a series of Early American Pattern Glass tableware names whose last syllable is "-tec." These higher quality patterns are: Aztec, Bontec, Carltec, Doltec, Fentec, Glentec, Martec, Nortec, Plutec, Plytec, Quintec, Rotec, Sextec, Startec, Toltec, Valtec, Wiltec, Wortec, and Yutec. Not until 1904 was McKee-Jeannette Glass Company was granted a patent for its Pres-Cut trademark, so the earliest "tec" patterns and pieces are unmarked; various markings were utilized in the years that followed. The most successful "tec" pattern was Fentec, with pieces of this pattern shown in McKee catalogues until 1942.

Corporate restructuring occurred in 1908 when the McKee Glass Company was born. "Tec" glassware was a large part of McKee Glass Company's product line with the addition of new patterns (see the list above) through 1915. In 1945, Kemple Glass Works purchased many of the "tec" molds and produced thirteen patterns of "tec" glassware until 1970. These were often in colors and in milk glass, none of which is original to the McKee production years. Wheaton acquired many of Kemple's molds when the Kemple Glass Works terminated operations in 1970, and continued the reproduction of "tec" glassware until 1979.

The reorganization of National Glass Company in 1908 also spawned the birth of the Cambridge Glass Company and the Indiana Glass Company.

McKee Glass Company and Cambridge Glass Company became licensed to manufacture specific lines of United States Glass Company and Duncan & Miller Glass Company glassware in 1916. A percentage of the profits from this product line of pressed, figured, and cut glassware that McKee (and Cambridge) created was given to U.S. Glass and Duncan & Miller.

In 1917 Glasbake Ovenware was introduced to compete with the highly successful PYREX® ovenware manufactured by Corning Glass Works. This clear, tempered glass was designed to withstand the hot temperatures of an oven and tolerate the chilly interior of an ice box. (Glasbake continued to be produced until 1983, long after the demise of McKee.)

Right: Early McKee Glass mantel clock shown in green, but also available in amber, amethyst, blue, and "canary." Sold as Tambour Art Glass, it is 14" long with a 4" dial. *Courtesy of Bob and Cindy Bentley.*

The Depression Years

The 1920s ushered in a new era of glassmaking. Indiana Glass Company introduced the Avocado pattern in colored glassware in 1923 and Fostoria offered colored glass dinnerware patterns in 1924, so a new trend for colored glass tableware had begun. The companies that quickly got involved in the production of colored glassware fared best during the Depression at the end of the decade, as they had already reconfigured their factories to meet the demand of American women who loved the new, colorful look that often included a "free" price tag.

Prior to the stock market crash in 1929, America was in a period of economic boom and many people had an abundance of disposable income. The glass industry was thriving and factories peppered the Ohio, West Virginia, and western Pennsylvania landscape where natural resources were abundant and local governments often provided financial incentives for manufacturing plants that provided jobs and revenue to the communities. The development of faster, more automatically-operated equipment brought a renaissance to the glass manufacturing industry. Now more than bottles, jars, and insulators could be easily created, including colored glass tableware that was available through some of the high quality glass producers. The pieces were well-made and sold through finer department stores. As the 1920s progressed, production had become so automated that as the country headed into the stock market crash of October, 1929, American factories with modern equipment had created a supply that exceeded demand, causing prices of manufactured goods to decline.

"In 1929, Yale University economist Irving Fisher stated confidently: 'The nation is marching along a permanently high plateau of prosperity.' Five days later, the bottom dropped out of the stock market and ushered in the Great Depression, the worst economic downturn in American history. Although Americans often believe that the Crash was the starting point of the Great Depression, many historians point out that it wasn't the sole cause." (http://us.history.wisc.edu/hist102/lectures/lecture18.html)

The swift American spiral into fiscal chaos was initiated in the Autumn of 1929. My father, a Philadelphian, spoke of several men on his block committing suicide, as they had lost everything: the family's wealth, the ability to earn a living, and the willingness to face another day.

My husband's family was largely rural, and West Virginian farmers at least maintained the ability to feed their families. As the land had been in his family for several generations, they did not face foreclosures that were rampant throughout the country. Also, their mountainous terrain shielded them from the 1930s Dust Bowl, when more than a hundred million acres of drought-ridden American farmland had its topsoil blown away in scores of wind storms with gusts exceeding fifty miles per hour.

"Brother, Can You Spare a Dime?" was more than a song, it was reality in America and abroad. The Great Depression caused many businesses to fail, and Depression Glass, as colored glass tableware became known, was a tool to entice Americans to spend what little money they had. Depression Glass was mass produced, poor quality glassware that was often available to consumers as a "free" premium gift with the purchase of a product or a service. Glassware was placed inside packages of food and soaps; it was given away with the purchase of a theater ticket; and it was free with the purchase of certain items, such as a magazine subscription or a quantity of seeds, and so forth.

McKee Glass Company is not usually thought of as a major player in Depression Glass, but several dinnerware patterns were produced by McKee. The most recognized patterns of Depression Glass created in McKee factories are limited to Rock Crystal Flower and Laurel, and both of these patterns are featured in the second part of this book. Rock Crystal Flower was introduced in crystal (clear) glass in 1921 so when colored glass became fashionable it was effortless for McKee to make the transition. Laurel, only available in opaque colors, was produced in the 1930s. Although among the first American glass producers to manufacture wares in color, McKee was one of the last to convert from handmade to machine-made glass.

Some of the lesser-known McKee dinnerware patterns included plain or blank glass with a scalloped edge and an eight-sided (octagonal) shape. Occasional pieces, such as bowls, covered jars, and boxes, were produced in the Brocade pattern in pink and green. Jade-ite, which McKee called "Skokie" green, luncheon sets were made, as well as a variety of water sets, dispensers, lamps, vases, and other forms. When compared with the options made by other glass manufacturers, McKee's dinnerware styles were limited.

Tumblers and razor hones colorfully illustration the rainbow of hues created by McKee Glass Company. *Courtesy of Randy Morey and Carol Miller.*

Kitchen Glass

The McKee Glass Company wares that became their successful offerings during the Depression era are those called "kitchen glass;" they are featured in the first part of this book. McKee Glass Company was the premiere manufacturer of opaque-colored glassware. Items in this category include glassware utilized to prepare, serve, and store food: canisters, refrigerator boxes, and mixing bowls are among the most common and recognizable. Not only did McKee Glass Company create a successful line of kitchen glass, they did so in opaque colors that are favorites with today's collectors. Seville, custard, chalaine, delphite, French Ivory, Poudre Blue, and jade-ite (which McKee called "Skokie" green) top the list. They were foremost producers of this colorful machine-made glassware for two decades.

One can summarize McKee's kitchen glass with the acronym "BORN," as follows:

B = Bell bowls
O = Opaque colors
R = Reuse molds
N = Nudes

Bell bowls refer to the shape of McKee Glass Company's most popular mixing bowls; when upside down, they resemble the shape of a bell. Although "normal" round bowls were produced, the bell-shaped bowl is a signature McKee creation, and was made in 6", 7", 8", and 9" diameters. There are a few 10" diameter bowls, but they are very few.

All glass companies exist to make a profit. During the Great Depression, it was exceedingly difficult to be profitable; using and reusing molds significantly lowered production costs. One can easily see evidence of the reuse of molds when comparing well-known Depression Glass patterns, such as Parrot and Madrid. They are patterns documented to have come from the same molds, and the utilization of molds in as many applications as possible was common and necessary. McKee Glass Company kitchen glassware designs were very limited, since the same molds were used again and again. The only changes made were the colors of the glass or surface decorations. McKee Glass Company produced the recognizable "Sunkist" orange reamer as well as a smaller reamer for lemons and a larger one for grapefruits. They were three sizes with many color variations. The molds were the same while the colors of the glass were not.

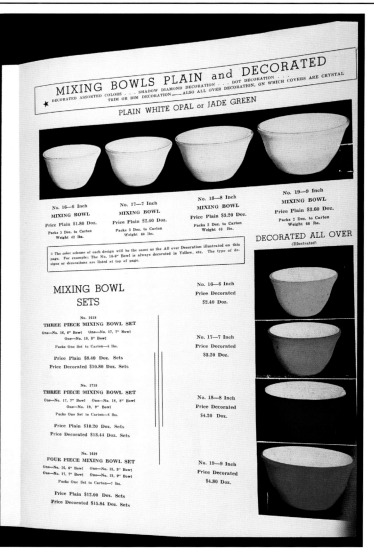

A page from McKee Glass Company's "McKee DeLuxe Kitchenware" catalogue number 39 shows the variety of decorations and colors available on the four different bell bowls created by the continual reuse of four mold designs. *Courtesy of Randy Morey and Carol Miller.*

Sunkist orange reamer. *Courtesy of Randy Morey and Carol Miller.*

The use of nude women as a decoration is one aspect of the Art Deco movement of the 1920s and 1930s. Glass companies attempted to provide that which was in vogue, so naturally glassware with nude women became readily available. Cambridge Glass Company is noted for their assortment of stemmed glassware featuring a nude woman as the stem. McKee Glass Company created nude vases that became jars and lamps (by reusing those molds), nude cocktail tumblers, and nude mugs. Today these are among the most prized of all kitchen glassware, no matter which manufacturer one is considering. Very few glassware nudes are found with their legs spread. This is discussed in greater detail, so keep reading. Glassware featuring ladies with their legs apart are higher in value than the same items with the legs together, simply because of a limited supply.

Later Years

Glassware for the kitchen continued to be produced into the 1940s and beyond. McKee Glass Company offered glass stovetop cookware that was in direct competition with PYREX® Flameware. They also produced children's tea sets called "Hostess Tea Sets" in the Laurel pattern. These were reminiscent of Hazel-Atlas Glass Company's Moderntone "Little Hostess Party Sets." Neither of the McKee lines was particularly successful.

Little documentation of McKee Glass Company endeavors in glassware for the home can be found after World War II. With roots in insulators and even early automobile lenses, McKee Glass Company was diversified enough to continue as an independent entity until 1951, when it became a subsidiary of Thatcher Glass Manufacturing Company. Thatcher had begun with the production of reusable glass milk bottles around the turn of the twentieth century. Technical glassware became the focus of this division – beakers, funnels, and so forth.

In 1961, Jeannette Glass Company purchased Thatcher and thereby acquired McKee, at least what was left if it. Some glass tableware continued to be manufactured until Jeannette's closure in 1983, when the factory closed.

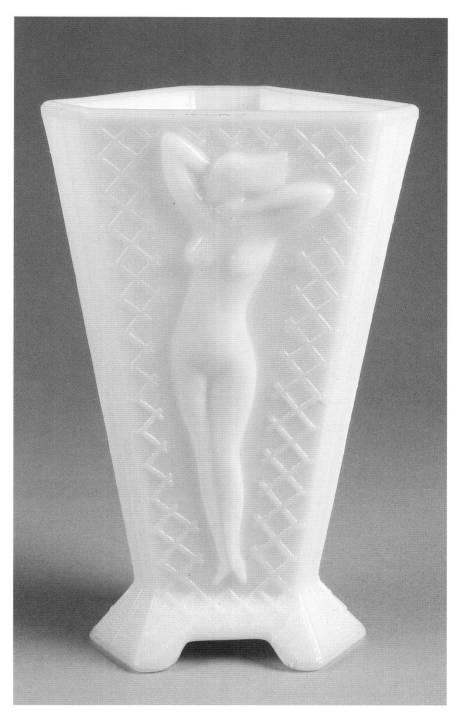

No. 100 "Triangle" vase rarely seen in white. *Courtesy of Todd Baum and Jesse Speicher.*

CLARIFICATION OF MCKEE KITCHEN GLASS ITEMS

Range Sets

The use of spices during the Depression years was a luxury few could afford. Preparing the basic meals was a challenge during a time when America's national annual income fell by about 50% from $2,300 to $1,500. Farm prices matched this figure as crops and meat prices declined about 50%. Farmers' incomes dropped from an average of $750 per year to $273 per year and the value of their land plummeted. Mother's cooking depended on salt, pepper, flour, and on rare occasions, sugar. As a matter of convenience manufacturers of stoves and ovens, called ranges, began to provide a place for these shakers. Sometimes this provision was a simple as an indent in the surface of the cook top,

A range set in "Seville" yellow. *Courtesy of Randy Morey and Carol Miller.*

but more elaborate configurations were available. These four shakers: salt, pepper, flour, sugar, became known as "range sets" as manufacturers standardized their size and shape. These shakers were often square-shaped as these simply required less space.

Later range sets might also include a drippings container. "Drippings" were the fat, oil, and grease accumulated during the cooking process. This liquid was an essential element for making soap, another task assigned to Mother, but during World War II this grease was used in the manufacture of explosives. Having a convenient, safe method to store drippings became a part of America's war effort.

A sampling of McKee Glass Company "Drippings" containers. Note that there are only three different molds featuring a variety of decorations. Drippings jars were made from canisters and refrigerator boxes by simply adding the word "Drippings." *Courtesy of Randy Morey and Carol Miller.*

Many configurations in three sizes, but all of these shakers feature the Roman Arch design. *Courtesy of Randy Morey and Carol Miller.*

Roman Arch Design

Many McKee shakers were molded with a curved motif on two sides known as the "Roman Arch" design. (Some collectors refer to this as Roman Arches.) Made in a variety of sizes and most often in the four most commonly-used shakers: salt, pepper, flour, sugar, Roman Arch pieces are usually marked on the bottom with the signature circle with McK inside and were shown in catalogues as the No. 37 shakers. Reproductions are found with a smooth base and no markings.

McKee Glass Company utilized a variety of lettering to differentiate the four shakers including names in script, names in printing, abbreviations of two letters and one letter in both script and printing, and so on. Shakers were even produced for use in French-speaking Quebec, Canada and can be found in these variations in the French language. Common in Canada, these shakers are quite popular with American collectors.

Roman Arch shakers were also decorated, as shown with these "Decorated Dots." Dots were also used on canisters, refrigerator boxes, bowls, and more. *Courtesy of Randy Morey and Carol Miller.*

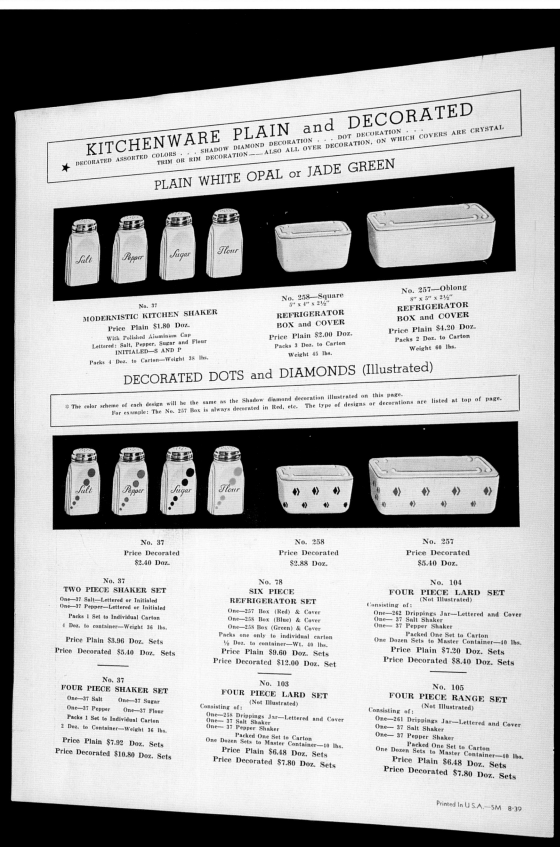

★ KITCHENWARE PLAIN and DECORATED
DECORATED ASSORTED COLORS . . . SHADOW DIAMOND DECORATION . . . DOT DECORATION . . .
TRIM OR RIM DECORATION—ALSO ALL OVER DECORATION, ON WHICH COVERS ARE CRYSTAL

PLAIN WHITE OPAL or JADE GREEN

No. 37
MODERNISTIC KITCHEN SHAKER
Price Plain $1.80 Doz.
With Polished Aluminum Cap
Lettered: Salt, Pepper, Sugar and Flour
INITIALED—S AND P
Packs 4 Doz. to Carton—Weight 38 lbs.

No. 258—Square
5" x 4" x 2½"
REFRIGERATOR BOX and COVER
Price Plain $2.00 Doz.
Packs 3 Doz. to Carton
Weight 45 lbs.

No. 257—Oblong
8" x 5" x 2½"
REFRIGERATOR BOX and COVER
Price Plain $4.20 Doz.
Packs 2 Doz. to Carton
Weight 60 lbs.

DECORATED DOTS and DIAMONDS (Illustrated)

✻ The color scheme of each design will be the same as the Shadow diamond decoration illustrated on this page.
For example: The No. 257 Box is always decorated in Red, etc. The type of designs or decorations are listed at top of page.

No. 37
Price Decorated
$2.40 Doz.

No. 258
Price Decorated
$2.88 Doz.

No. 257
Price Decorated
$5.40 Doz.

No. 37
TWO PIECE SHAKER SET
One—37 Salt—Lettered or Initialed
One—37 Pepper—Lettered or Initialed
Packs 1 Set to Individual Carton
4 Doz. to container—Weight 36 lbs.

Price Plain $3.96 Doz. Sets
Price Decorated $5.40 Doz. Sets

No. 78
SIX PIECE REFRIGERATOR SET
One—257 Box (Red) & Cover
One—258 Box (Blue) & Cover
One—258 Box (Green) & Cover
Packs one only to individual carton
½ Doz. to container—Wt. 40 lbs.
Price Plain $9.60 Doz. Sets
Price Decorated $12.00 Doz. Set

No. 104
FOUR PIECE LARD SET
(Not Illustrated)
Consisting of:
One—262 Drippings Jar—Lettered and Cover
One—37 Salt Shaker
One—37 Pepper Shaker
Packed One Set to Carton
One Dozen Sets to Master Container—40 lbs.
Price Plain $7.20 Doz. Sets
Price Decorated $8.40 Doz. Sets

No. 37
FOUR PIECE SHAKER SET
One—37 Salt   One—37 Sugar
One—37 Pepper   One—37 Flour
Packs 1 Set to Individual Carton
2 Doz. to Container—Weight 36 lbs.
Price Plain $7.92 Doz. Sets
Price Decorated $10.80 Doz. Sets

No. 103
FOUR PIECE LARD SET
(Not Illustrated)
Consisting of:
One—258 Drippings Jar—Lettered and Cover
One—37 Salt Shaker
One—37 Pepper Shaker
Packed One Set to Carton
One Dozen Sets to Master Container—10 lbs.
Price Plain $6.48 Doz. Sets
Price Decorated $7.80 Doz. Sets

No. 105
FOUR PIECE RANGE SET
(Not Illustrated)
Consisting of:
One—261 Drippings Jar—Lettered and Cover
One—37 Salt Shaker
One—37 Pepper Shaker
Packed One Set to Carton
One Dozen Sets to Master Container—10 lbs.
Price Plain $6.48 Doz. Sets
Price Decorated $7.80 Doz. Sets

Printed In U.S.A.—5M 8-39

A catalogue page provides information regarding the marketing of McKee kitchen glass. Decorated items were much higher in price than their plain counterparts. Roman Arch shakers are described as "modernistic." *Courtesy of Randy Morey and Carol Miller.*

Here are seven variations of the salt shaker in French Ivory. From left to right: square shaker with large Deco lettering, square shaker with small Deco lettering and red trim at the top, square shaker with small Deco lettering, Roman Arch shaker with red trim at the top, plain Roman Arch shaker, Roman Arch shaker with "S" for salt and red trim at top, plain Roman Arch shaker with "S" for salt. *Courtesy of Randy Morey and Carol Miller.*

Most lids are metal, but some shaker lids were created in red and black Bakelite which add to the value. Bakelite lids often but not always have holes arranged in letters "P" for pepper and "S" for salt.

Metal shaker lids are found in three main designs. Original metal lids for Roman Arch shakers are often "stacked" in design with a wider base and narrower top and were machined with fifteen holes while reproduction lids have nineteen holes. Another design has the lid almost totally flat with ridges along the outer edge, presumably to assist in gripping when opening a shaker. The hardest-to-find lid is the "puffy" lid which simply looks like the name says, puffy. These lids were very susceptible to damage and few survived in pristine condition. The values shown for shakers in this book assume the lids as well as the glass bases are in perfect condition.

McKee Glass Company never produced shakers for the now-common spices utilized in contemporary recipes such as Basil and Oregano.

There was one canister made with the Roman Arch design, a white sugar canister.

This Bakelite lid was designed for use on a salt shaker. *Courtesy of Randy Morey and Carol Miller.*

Decorations

Although McKee Glass Company utilized many of the same molds again and again, variations are abundant as not only did the color of the glass change, so did the surface decorations. An extra step in the creation of this kitchen glass involved firing on colors in stripes, bows, circles, sailboats, and so on, and these are among the most prized pieces of McKee kitchen glass. Many of these decorations were applied to a variety of pieces allowing one to acquire sets that matched: refrigerator boxes, shakers, bowls, canisters, etc., things that are of the most interest to contemporary collectors.

The Roman Arch sugar canister with a vintage decal covering the original lettering. *Courtesy of Randy Morey and Carol Miller.*

To clarify the molds most frequently used in McKee kitchen items, some measurements are provided:
- **Refrigerator boxes** were most often 4" x 5" and 5" x 8".
- **Round canisters with glass lids** came in three main heights: 2.5", 3.5", and 4.5".
- **Canisters** - on rare occasions one will find a 5" tall canister.
- **Canisters with a screw lid** are usually 6.25" tall or 7.5" tall.
- **Canisters with a press-on lid** are 7.5" tall.
- **Footed tumbler** 4.25" tall was also an **egg cup**.

"Nude" Tumblers and More

McKee Glass Company produced a variety of glassware incorporating a nude female into the design. Among the most sought-after nude glassware is the bottoms-up tumbler made with a rounded base which is the lady's tushie. The only way one can stand a bottoms-up tumbler on a table is if it is upside down, so the user is compelled to drink the entirety of the contents before placing it on a table hence "Bottoms up!"

Produced in the 1930s, the bottoms-up tumbler design was not original to McKee; it was copied from pottery tumblers created by White Cloud Farms of Rock Tavern, New York. Will Low Bacher held the patent (77,725) for these split-legged tumblers since February 19, 1929. McKee's production was a violation of Bacher's patent and he and White Cloud Farms launched a suit against this blatant infringement. The case was settled out of court when McKee bought the patent and reconfigured their design by bringing the legs together.

Bottoms-up tumblers were perfect for use during Prohibition, a time when many Americans continued to imbibe often seeking to achieve the glamour portrayed by lavish Hollywood productions. The nude Flapper draped over a tumbler offered a great deal of appeal and McKee continued their production offering the glasses separately and in sets of four.

The McKee Glass Company catalogue offered kitchen glassware that was plain, trimmed with color, and decorated. *Courtesy of Randy Morey and Carol Miller.*

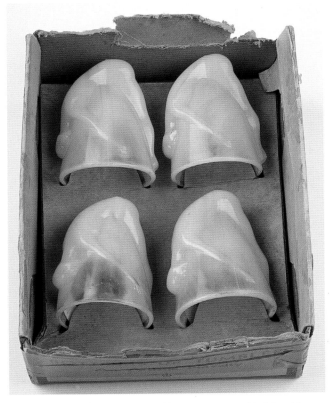

Set of four opalescent caramel bottoms-up cocktail tumblers in an original box. *Courtesy of Faye and Robert Smith.*

The use of nude females was also incorporated into "Triangle" vases made in several sizes. Vases became candy jars when covered and the basis of a lamp when the small round depression on the bottom was machined open. None are easily found and all are in great demand.

Additional Non-shaker Lid Clarification

Canisters, refrigerator boxes, and drippings jars were produced utilizing a variety of lid designs as listed below:
- glass lids were the same color of glass as the base
- glass lids were a different color of glass than the base creating a dramatic contrast
- glass lids were clear although the base was opaque
- metal lids screwed onto the base
- metal lids snapped or pressed onto the base (referred to as "press-on" in this book)

Two-cup Measures

Three different molds were utilized for the two-cup measure. Shown side by side the dissimilar characteristics become easy to detect. The measure on the left is the most recent mold and pieces are found with the McK symbol and/or the Glasbake name. The measure on the right appears to be a transitional design between the earliest one shown in the middle and the newest one on the left.

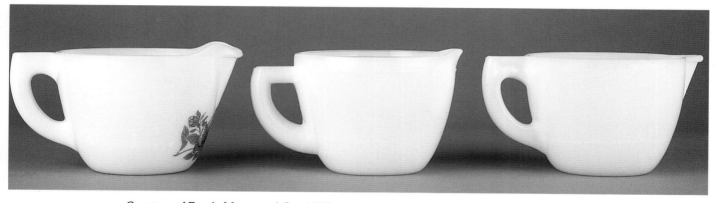

Courtesy of Randy Morey and Carol Miller.

Part One
Kitchen Glass by Color

BLACK KITCHEN GLASS, PLAIN OR UNDECORATED

8.5" console bowl, $100. *Courtesy of John and Marilyn Yallop.*

7.25" + bowl, $100. *Courtesy of Randy Morey and Carol Miller*

3" x 2.25" razor hone, $20. *Courtesy of Randy Morey and Carol Miller.*

Bottoms up cocktail tumbler with the earlier split leg design that originally sold for $1.00. $225. *Courtesy of Todd Baum and Jesse Spreicher.*

Sunkist orange reamer, $750. *Courtesy of Arnie Masoner.*

Roman Arch shakers with rare vertical lettering. A flour shaker was made and four shakers would create a range set. $120 each. *Courtesy of Arnie Masoner.*

Roman Arch shakers, four with names in script and two with initials. $65 each. *Courtesy of Arnie Masoner.*

Roman Arch variation with Deco letters. $75 each if perfect. *Courtesy of Arnie Masoner.*

Square shakers with Deco lettering. $75 each if perfect. *Courtesy of Arnie Masoner.*

Square shakers introduced by McKee Glass Company as the "4 Piece Kitchen Shaker Set" for $1.40 in 1931. The value of these shakers is dependent on the quality of the lettering and the condition of the original metal tops as well as the condition of the glass. Salt, $70; pepper, $50; flour and sugar, $85. *Courtesy of Tom Donlan.*

Sterilizer jar, $200; 3.75" tall tumblers, $50 each; 3" x 2.25" razor hone, $20. *Courtesy of Randy Morey and Carol Miller.*

8.5" tall no. 100 triangle vases and a 7.5" tall vase with a lid and therefore a candy jar. Variations in height and nude versus dressed add to the values of these elusive vases. They can also be found with a hole in the bottom for conversion to a lamp. These vases were introduced in 1931. 8.5" tall, $275; 7.5" tall, $200; lid, $225. *Courtesy of Todd Baum and Jesse Spreicher.*

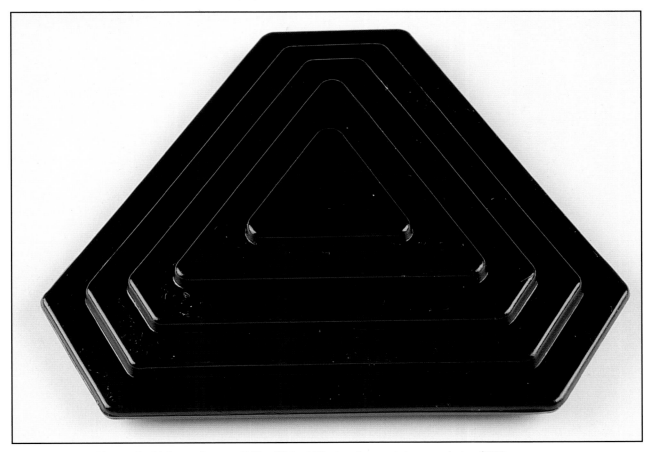

The stacked lid transforms a 7.5" tall No. 100 triangle vase into a candy jar. $225.
Courtesy of Todd Baum and Jesse Spreicher.

8" tall Sarah vase with planters from the early 1930s. Left to right the measurements for the planters are: 3.25" deep, 7" diameter no. 26 Bulb Bowl; 2.25" deep, 7" diameter No. 27 Bulb bowl; 5.25" deep, 6" diameter No. 25 Three-Footed Jardinière which becomes a cookie jar with the addition of a lid. *Courtesy of Todd Baum and Jesse Spreicher.*

5" x 9" x 3' deep window box planter. $125.
Courtesy of Todd Baum and Jesse Spreicher.

BLACK KITCHEN GLASS WITH RED TRIM

Four Roman Arch shakers with elusive Deco details, $150 each. *Courtesy of Randy Morey and Carol Miller.*

Roman Arch shaker with Gothic initial, $75. *Courtesy of Randy Morey and Carol Miller.*

Roman Arch shakers, four with names in script and two with painted lids and initials. $65 each. *Courtesy of Randy Morey and Carol Miller.*

Blue Kitchen Glass — Chalaine

Canisters left to right: 6.5" tall, $90; 4.5" tall, $90; 3.5" tall without lid, $20; with lid, $60.
Courtesy of Randy Morey and Carol Miller.

Back row: four 7.5" tall square canisters with screw-on lids originally sold for $2.50 for the set, now $600 for cereal, $500 each for tea, coffee, flour; front row: canister base, $50 as shown but with a name and lid the value would be $1200; square shakers, $175 each.
Courtesy of Randy Morey and Carol Miller.

Above: The orange reamer on the left originally sold for $.40 and is now worth $400. A grapefruit reamer is on the right, $800. *Courtesy of Arnie Masoner.*

Left to right: egg cup, $12; 6" tall four-cup measure originally sold as a batter jug for $.60, $500; 2.5" tall tumbler, $30; 5" tall base to an unknown item, $75. *Courtesy of Randy Morey and Carol Miller.*

Saucer, $10. This is an enigma as a cup has yet to be documented. If there is a cup for this saucer the value of the saucer would be greatly enhanced. *Courtesy of Randy Morey and Carol Miller.*

8" tall Sarah vase, $175. *Courtesy of Todd Baum and Jesse Spreicher.*

7.75" tall, 7.75" diameter "Modern Square" vase, $450. *Courtesy of Todd Baum and Jesse Spreicher.*

Nude and dressed No. 100 triangle vases with 5.5" diameter, 2.25" deep No. 26 bulb bowl. Vases, Nude vase, $600; dressed vase, $750; bulb bowl, $85. *Courtesy of Todd Baum and Jesse Spreicher.*

Blue Kitchen Glass — Cobalt

This triangle vase is the single most valuable item in this book as it is thought to be the only one made. Supposedly a factory worker made this and stealthily carried it home in his lunch pail. This is too rare to price. *Courtesy of Todd Baum and Jesse Spreicher.*

BLUE KITCHEN GLASS – DELPHITE

Bell bowls with vertical ribs, an uncommon design. 9", $175; 8", $150; 7" and 6", $125 each.
Courtesy of Randy Morey and Carol Miller.

5.5" tall coffee canister, $275; one-pound butter dish, $275; and Roman Arch shakers, $200 each.
Courtesy of Randy Morey and Carol Miller.

Four 6.25" tall square canisters with screw-on lids. $300 each.
Courtesy of Randy Morey and Carol Miller.

5.5" tall coffee canister, $275; 3" x 2.25" razor hone, $45; 3.75" tall tumbler, $150;
4.25" diameter "Cocotte" bowl, $100. *Courtesy of Randy Morey and Carol Miller.*

Roman Arch shakers,
$200 each. *Courtesy of
Randy Morey and Carol
Miller.*

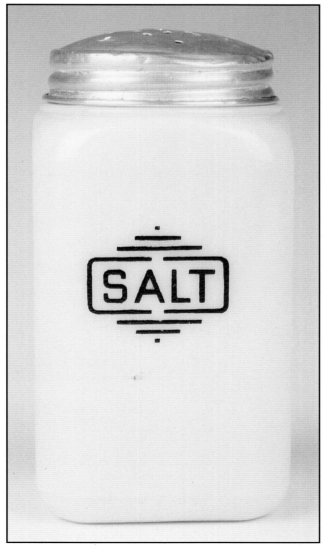

Square shaker with
Deco lettering. $175.
*Courtesy of Randy
Morey and Carol
Miller.*

Blue Kitchen Glass — Peacock

Many glass companies utilized this dramatic color, but McKee Glass Company was not one of those companies. The sole item in this book in this lovely hue is an 8.5" tall No. 100 triangle vase which features a dressed woman; usually these figures are nude. This is an *extremely* rare item. $1000. *Courtesy of Todd Baum and Jesse Spreicher.*

CARAMEL KITCHEN GLASS

5.5" deep three-footed No. 25 jardinière in a color McKee Glass Company called "Old Rose." $95. *Courtesy of Tom Donlan.*

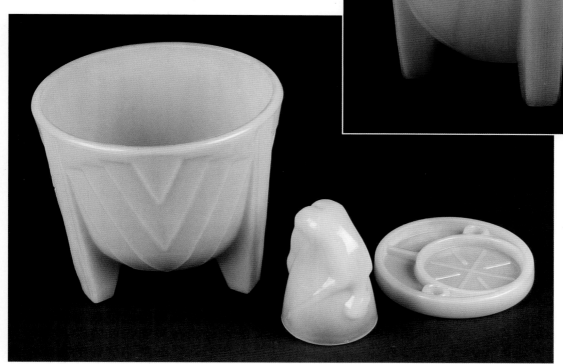

5.5" deep three-footed No. 25 jardinière in a color McKee Glass Company called "Old Rose" but clearly a different hue than the other jardinière, $95; bottoms up cocktail tumbler, $175; coaster for tumbler, $175. *Courtesy of Todd Baum and Jesse Spreicher.*

Original box (albeit taped and tattered) of bottoms up cocktail tumblers. The side panel reads: "IDEAL PRIZE FOR (can't discern this word) CARD PARTIES, CARNIVALS, PICNICS, ETC. THE TUMBLER WITH A BOTTOM BUT *TRY* TO MAKE IT STAND. BOTTOMS UP TUMBLER An artistic Novelty." $125 each; add $35 for the box in "as is" condition. *Courtesy of Faye and Robert Smith.*

Crystal Satinized or Frosted Kitchen Glass

A Roman Arch shaker that is rarely found in this color but is in low demand. $45. *Courtesy of Randy Morey and Carol Miller.*

Fired-On Kitchen Glass

4" diameter, 2.5" deep canister. $25. *Courtesy of Randy Morey and Carol Miller.*

Bell bowls with original box. Bowls, $25 each; box, $50.

FRENCH IVORY KITCHEN GLASS, PLAIN OR UNDECORATED

Four bell bowls in diameters of 9", 8", 7", 6". $25 each.
Courtesy of Randy Morey and Carol Miller.

Four round bowls in diameters of 11.5", 9", 7.25", 4.25". The smallest bowl is referred to
as a "Cocotte" bowl. $25 each. *Courtesy of Randy Morey and Carol Miller.*

6" diameter salt box with a metal lid, $200; 4.75" diameter swirled cracker bowl, $150; 8.5"
diameter scalloped-edge serving bowl, $65. *Courtesy of Randy Morey and Carol Miller.*

Almost 3" diameter butter pats. $65 each. *Courtesy of Randy Morey and Carol Miller.*

Red lettering is much less common than black lettering. This canister is 5" tall and 5.75" in diameter. *Courtesy of Randy Morey and Carol Miller.*

7.25" tall square coffee canister with a press down lid. $250. *Courtesy of Randy Morey and Carol Miller.*

7.25" tall canisters with press down lids, $250 each. *Courtesy of Randy Morey and Carol Miller.*

Four 6.25" tall square canisters with lids that screw into place. Note the color variations which are quite normal. $100 each. *Courtesy of Randy Morey and Carol Miller.*

Three 7.5" tall square canisters with lids that screw into place. $100 each. *Courtesy of Randy Morey and Carol Miller.*

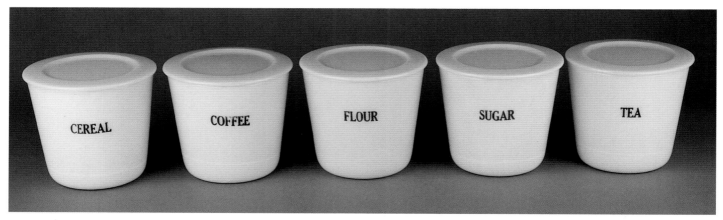

Five 5.5" tall round canisters with glass lids, all with printed names. $125 each. *Courtesy of Randy Morey and Carol Miller.*

A 7.75" tall "Column Canister" is the most rare and most valuable canister design. The variations in color are evident when comparing the coffee and tea canisters. $1000+ *Courtesy of Randy Morey and Carol Miller.*

A coaster is on the left; a butter pat is on the right. The coaster is a little larger and includes rays of glass to elevate a tumbler above any condensation that might have collected. Coaster, $125; butter pat, $65. *Courtesy of Randy Morey and Carol Miller.*

A coaster holder is among the rarest items in this book. $500. *Courtesy of Randy Morey and Carol Miller.*

Coasters are stored inside the holder/container until needed. These are elusive pieces. Holder, $500; coasters, $125 each; tumbler, $45. *Courtesy of Randy Morey and Carol Miller.*

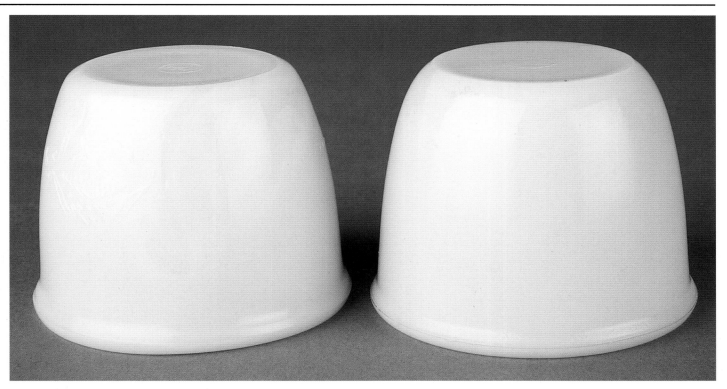

Custard cups, $20 each. *Courtesy of Randy Morey and Carol Miller.*

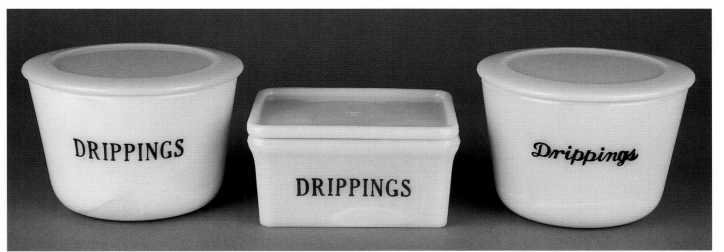

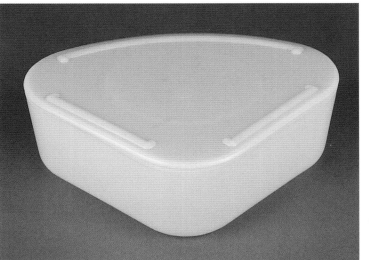

Above: Drippings jars illustrate how McKee Glass Company used the same molds again and again. The round jars are 3.5" tall canisters with printed and script names; the center drippings jar is a refrigerator box. $175 each. *Courtesy of Randy Morey and Carol Miller.*

The wedge refrigerator box is quite rare. $200. *Courtesy of Randy Morey and Carol Miller.*

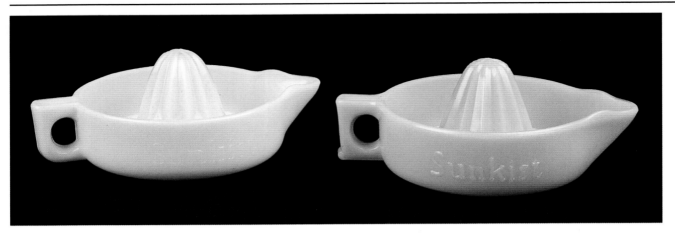

Inconsistencies in color formulation were the norm for McKee Glass Company and other manufacturers of glassware of this era. Today we are left with a rainbow of colors with boundless variations. Difficulties arise when we attempt to label some pieces as illustrated with these orange reamers. Some collectors and dealers will view the reamer on the right as caramel while others, like this author, consider it custard. This deeper color is much more in demand as it is less common, and this positively affects its value. Lighter reamer, $65; darker reamer, $200. *Courtesy of Randy Morey and Carol Miller.*

Two orange reamers and two lemon reamers. The orange reamers are virtually identical except one is marked and the other is not. The lemon reamer on the left (second from right) has a pointy reamer/cone and is not marked while the reamer on the right has a rounded reamer/cone and is marked "McK." $65 each. *Courtesy of Randy Morey and Carol Miller.*

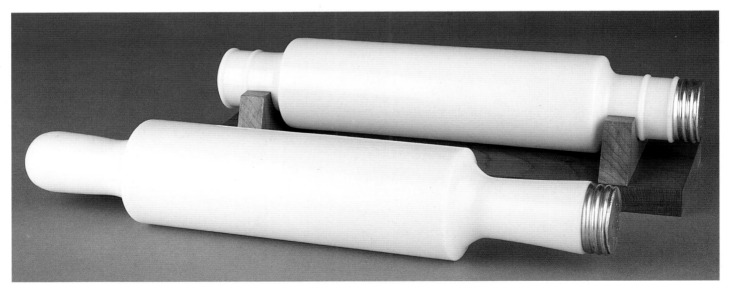

Rolling pins. Left/front: smooth handles, right/back: ridged handles, $225 each. *Courtesy of Randy Morey and Carol Miller.*

Roman Arch salt and pepper shakers with initials for salt and pepper, $45 each.
Courtesy of Arnie Masoner.

Roman Arch salt and pepper shakers with words in script, $45 each.
Courtesy of Arnie Masoner.

Square shakers with large Deco lettering in red, $60. *Courtesy of Todd Baum and Jesse Spreicher.*

Square shakers with large Deco lettering, $50 each. *Courtesy of John and Marilyn Yallop.*

Square shakers with flat and "puffy" lids and small Deco lettering. *Courtesy of Arnie Masoner.*

Six square shakers with small Deco lettering. Salt, pepper, flour, $50; others $60. *Courtesy of Todd Baum and Jesse Spreicher.*

Three hard-to-find versions of the square flour shaker, $100 each. *Courtesy of Randy Morey and Carol Miller.*

Snack tray/child's feeding dish, $40; 11" diameter tray with tab handles, $45; 5" x 7" oval baking dish, $25. *Courtesy of Randy Morey and Carol Miller.*

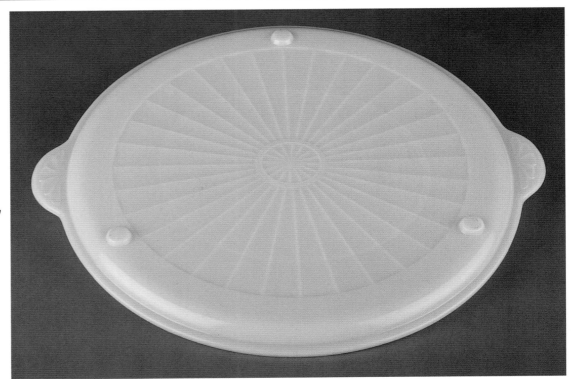

The underside of the 11" tray reveals three small feet and a starburst motif. *Courtesy of Randy Morey and Carol Miller.*

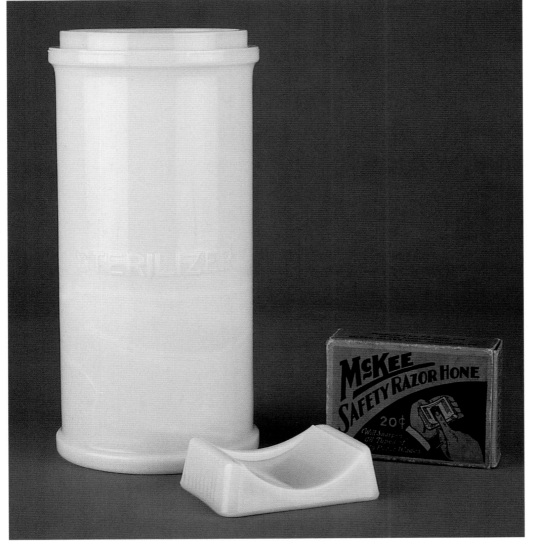

Embossed sterilizer jar (lid is missing) and 3" x 2.25" razor hone with original box. Jar as shown, $50; $125 with lid; razor hone, $20; add $20 for box. *Courtesy of Randy Morey and Carol Miller.*

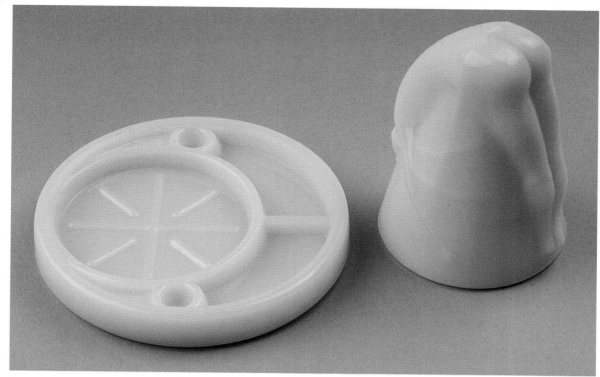

Bottoms up cocktail tumbler, $150; with coaster, $125. Note: Look for patent number 77725 on vintage bottoms up tumblers. *Courtesy of Todd Baum and Jesse Spreicher.*

Water dispensers. Left: 5" tall with small round lid, $250; right: 4" tall with large rectangular lid, $300. *Courtesy of Randy Morey and Carol Miller.*

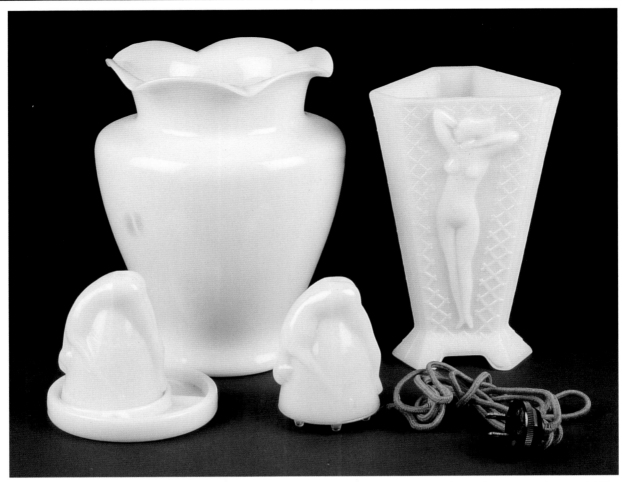

Right to left: 3.25" tall bottoms up cocktail tumbler, $150; on coaster, $125; $8" tall Sarah vase, $100; lighter fashioned from a cocktail tumbler, $250; 7.5" tall No. 100 triangle vase, $350. *Courtesy of Todd Baum and Jesse Spreicher.*

Underside of lighter fashioned from a bottoms up cocktail tumbler.
Courtesy of Todd Baum and Jesse Spreicher.

FRENCH IVORY KITCHEN GLASS
WITH DECORATED DOTS

Contemporary collectors refer the polka dotted glassware in this section as "Dots," but the actual name at the time of its manufacture was "Decorated Dot." McKee Glass Company marketed two-piece shaker sets consisting of salt and pepper which wholesaled for $5.40 for a dozen sets. This may seem inexpensive, but consider the cost of twelve plain Roman Arch shakers: $3.96.

Catalogues feature black, blue, red, and yellow, but green and orange is also presented.

Three 4.5" canisters celebrate the vibrancy of Decorated Dot. $200 each. *Courtesy of Randy Morey and Carol Miller.*

Black Decorated Dots

Roman Arch shakers, $125 each if perfect; these show wear. *Courtesy of Randy Morey and Carol Miller.*

2.5" tall canister on 5" x 8" refrigerator box and 4.5" canister. $200 each.
Courtesy of Randy Morey and Carol Miller.

Blue Decorated Dots

Four bell bowls, $200 each.
Courtesy of Randy Morey and Carol Miller.

Roman Arch pepper shaker, $200.
Courtesy of Randy Morey and Carol Miller.

Left to right: 5" canister, $250; 2.5" canister, $200; 3.5" canister, $225; Roman Arch sugar shaker, $175; 5" x 8" refrigerator box, $200. *Courtesy of Randy Morey and Carol Miller.*

Green Decorated Dots

4.5" tall canister on 5" x 8" refrigerator box and 9" scalloped-edged bowl, $250 each. *Courtesy of Randy Morey and Carol Miller.*

4" Roman Arch shakers, $200 each. *Courtesy of Randy Morey and Carol Miller.*

7" canisters with screw lids, $225 each. *Courtesy of Randy Morey and Carol Miller.*

Two-cup measure. $200. *Courtesy of Randy Morey and Carol Miller.*

5" x 8" refrigerator box and 8.5" scalloped-rimmed serving bowl, $200 each. *Courtesy of Randy Morey and Carol Miller.*

Orange Decorated Dots

Left to right: 4" x 5" refrigerator box, $300; Roman Arch shakers, $250 each; 7" and 8" bell bowls, $250 each. *Courtesy of Randy Morey and Carol Miller.*

Four Roman Arch shakers, $250 each; 4" x 5" refrigerator box, $300. *Courtesy of Arnie Masoner.*

Mixed Colors of Decorated Dots

Roman Arch shakers with orange dots are more difficult to find than shakers with red dots. Orange, $250 each; red, $125 each. *Courtesy of Arnie Masoner*

Red Dots

Left to right: 3.5" tall canister without a lid, $100 if complete; 4.5" canister, $200; drippings jar, $250; 2.5" tall canister with red trim, $200. *Courtesy of Arnie Masoner.*

Left to right: 2.5" canister, 7.5" tall tea canister with screw lid, 3.5" canister on 4.5" canister, two-cup measure on 4" x 5" refrigerator box, $200 each. *Courtesy of Randy Morey and Carol Miller.*

Left to right: one-pound butter dish, $200; tea canister with screw lid, $200; 4" x 5" refrigerator box, $200; on drippings jar, $600; on 5" x 8" refrigerator box, $200. *Courtesy of Arnie Masoner.*

Roman Arch shakers. This set of four is a "Range Set." $125 each. *Courtesy of Randy Morey and Carol Miller.*

FRENCH IVORY KITCHEN GLASS WITH DIAMONDS

Left to right: 3.5"
tall canister, 4" x 5"
refrigerator boxes on 5"
x 8" refrigerator box, and
Roman Arch shakers.
$200 each. *Courtesy of
Tom Donlan.*

Rare
drippings
jar. $350.
*Courtesy
of Tom
Donlan.*

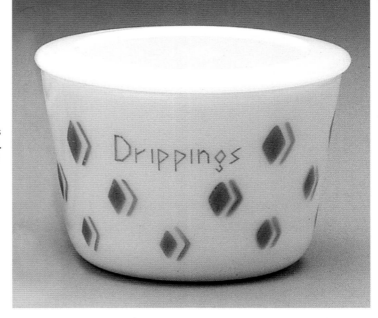

Below: Back row: 4.5" tall
canister, two-cup measure;
front row: 6" bell bowl, 4" x
5" refrigerator box on 5" x
8" refrigerator box, Roman
Arch shakers. $200 each.
Courtesy of Tom Donlan.

FRENCH IVORY KITCHEN GLASS WITH HAND PAINTED DETAILS

A "Range Set" with red Deco lettering with hand painted flowers. $125 each. *Courtesy of Tom Donlan.*

FRENCH IVORY KITCHEN GLASS WITH TRIM

Trim can be as simple as a subtle addition of a line of color that is fired onto the glass when the "S" for salt is added. *Courtesy of Randy Morey and Carol Miller.*

8" and 9" bell bowls with orange trim; $65 each. *Courtesy of Randy Morey and Carol Miller.*

The pronounced red trim of these pieces enhances their value. Left to right: 3.5" canister on 4.5" canister, $150 each; 7", 8", and 9" bell bowls, $75 each; rare drippings jar, $200. *Courtesy of Randy Morey and Carol Miller.*

Left to right: 2 cup measure, $125; refrigerator boxes, $125 each; flour shaker with Deco lettering, $125; 9" diameter serving bowl, $125; salt shaker with Deco lettering, $115; pepper shaker with Deco lettering, $85. *Courtesy of Randy Morey and Carol Miller.*

One-pound butter dishes were sold as "Covered Butter Boxes" which originally sold for fifty cents. The butter dish without trim has the following measurements: base: 8.5" handle to handle x 4"; cover: 7" x 3.25" x 2.5" deep. The green trim enhances the value of a butter dish that measures: base: 6.5" handle to handle x 3.5"; cover: 6" x 3.5" x 2.5" deep. Both covers have the daisy-like motif found on McKee butter covers. Plain, $100; trimmed, $150. *Courtesy of Todd Baum and Jesse Spreicher.*

One-pound butter dish with green trim, the larger size with a base measuring 8.5" handle to handle x 4" and a cover measuring: 7" x 3.25" x 2.5" deep. The two-cup measure also features green trim. Butter dish, $150; measuring cup, $125. *Courtesy of Randy Morey and Carol Miller.*

Roman Arch shakers with red trim. $100 each. *Courtesy of Arnie Masoner.*

Roman Arch salt and pepper shakers in two sizes. The shakers in the middle have a fine line of trim in black. $45 each. *Courtesy of Randy Morey and Carol Miller.*

GREEN KITCHEN GLASS

Satinized or Frosted

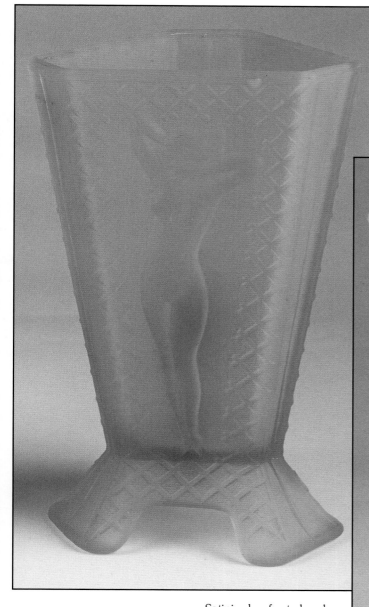

Satinized or frosted nude glassware is quite elusive. Shown are two 8.5" triangle vases. $350 each. *Courtesy of Todd Baum and Jesse Spreicher.*

Skokie Green (Jade-ite) Kitchen Glass

Pinched decanter and water bottle designed for ease in lifting. $250 each. *Courtesy of John and Marilyn Yallop.*

Below: Left to right: 5" x 7" oval baking dish, $50; 4.25" diameter round Cocotte bowl, $85; 4.25" diameter egg beater bowl with spout, $85; 6.25"+ mixer bowl without spout, $75. *Courtesy of Randy Morey and Carol Miller.*

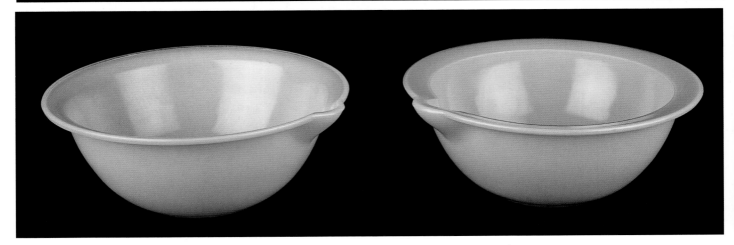

Batter bowls with pouring spouts. Left: curved rim, $75; right: flat rim, $125.
Courtesy of Randy Morey and Carol Miller.

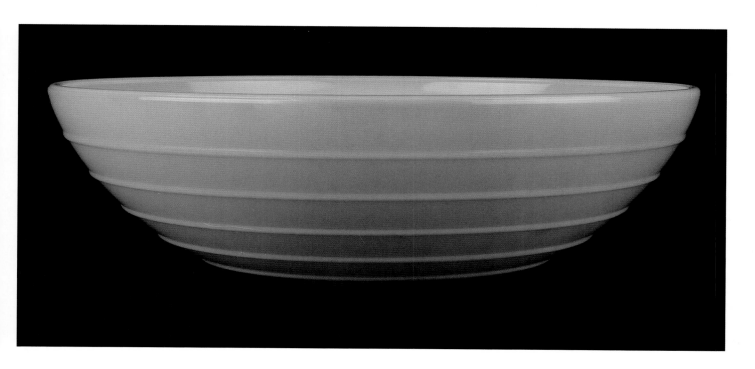

Rare 8" diameter ridged bowl, $200. *Courtesy of Randy Morey and Carol Miller.*

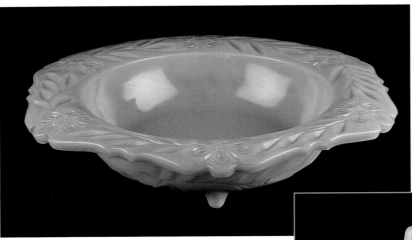

Decorative bowl reminiscent
of McKee Glass Company's
roots. $250. *Courtesy of John
and Marilyn Yallop.*

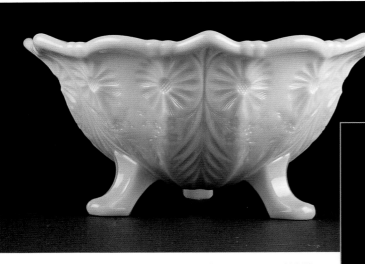

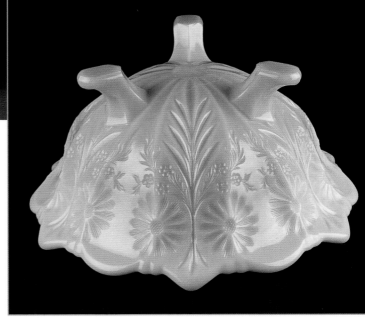

Decorative bowl reminiscent of McKee
Glass Company's roots. $250. *Cour-
tesy of John and Marilyn Yallop.*

Two console bowls in the "Autumn" pattern. $125 each.
Courtesy of John and Marilyn Yallop.

Candle holders in the "Autumn" pattern. $75 each.
Courtesy of John and Marilyn Yallop.

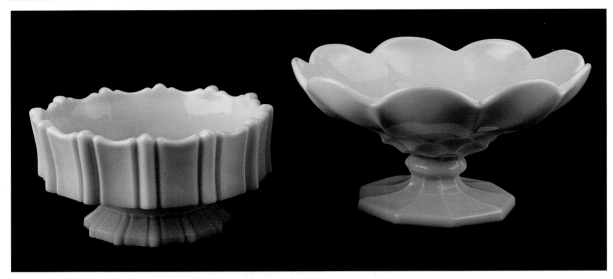

Candy dishes/ comports. The piece on the right is known to be McKee; the one on the right features McKee characteristics, but may not be McKee. Left: 4.5" tall, 8" diameter; right: 5" tall, 10.5" diameter. $125 each. *Courtesy of Randy Morey and Carol Miller.*

Round canisters were created in a variety of sizes. Those without labels were intended to be refrigerator boxes. *Courtesy of Randy Morey and Carol Miller.*

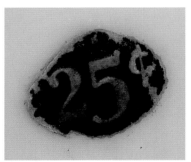

Cereal canister with screw lid. 7.5" tall. Original price tag remains. $200. Add $25 for the price tag. *Courtesy of Randy Morey and Carol Miller.*

Canisters with screw lids. 7.5" tall. $200 each. *Courtesy of Randy Morey and Carol Miller.*

4.5" tall, 3.5" tall, 2.5" tall canisters. Left to right: $100, $80, $60. *Courtesy of John and Marilyn Yallop.*

A 7.75" tall "Column Canister" is the most rare and most valuable canister design. $1000+ *Courtesy of Linda and Ron Peterson.*

Almost 3.25" in diameter, the coaster (left) features elevated ridges of glass which allow a tumbler to be above any condensation that might collect thus reducing drips of water when the tumbler is lifted. A butter pat is on the right. $50 each. *Courtesy of Randy Morey and Carol Miller.*

Custard cups. Left: plain, $35; right: design, $45. *Courtesy of Randy Morey and Carol Miller.*

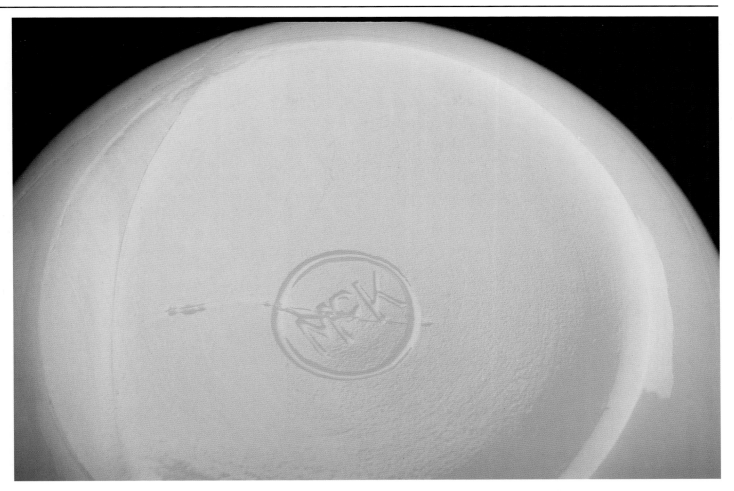

The McKee Glass Company logo is easy to see on the bottom of a custard cup. Most kitchen glass is marked with this symbol. *Courtesy of Randy Morey and Carol Miller.*

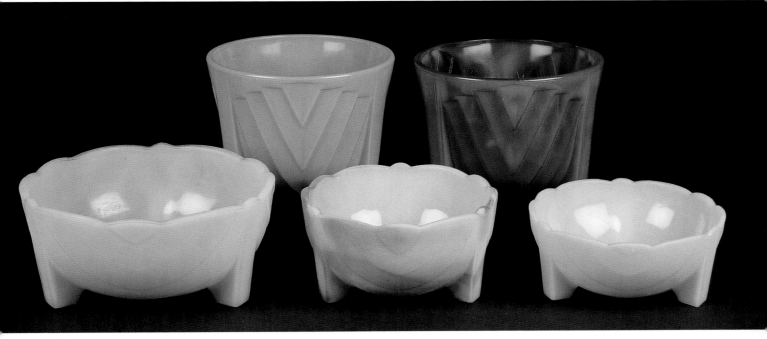

Jardinières and bulb bowls introduced by McKee Glass Company in 1931 that clearly show the lack of consistency when formulating jade-ite glassware. Back row: two 6" diameter, 5.5" deep, three-footed No. 25 jardinières; front row: three different bulb bowls measuring 7" diameter, 3.25" deep; 5.5" diameter, 2.75" deep; and 5.5" diameter, 2.5" deep. $125 each. *Courtesy of Todd Baum and Jesse Speicher.*

Rare goblet, $175. *Courtesy of John and Marilyn Yallop.*

When a lid is added to a smooth-rimmed No. 25 three-footed jardinière a cookie jar is created. Base, $125; lid, $175. *Courtesy of Todd Baum and Jesse Speicher.*

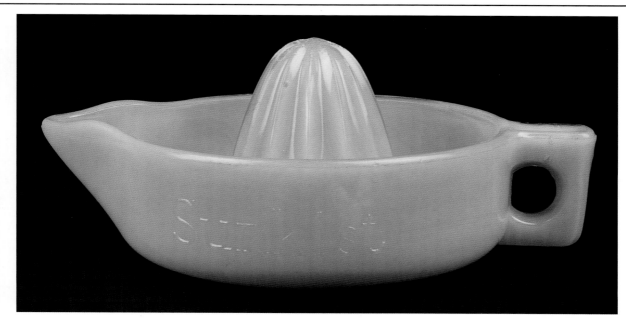

Sunkist orange reamer. $50. *Courtesy of Randy Morey and Carol Miller.*

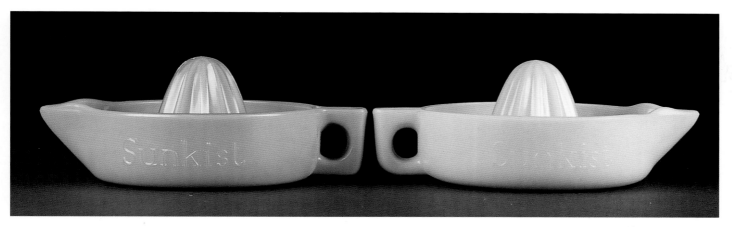

Above: It is interesting to note the different shades of green that were produced. Collectors tend to prefer darker greens. *Courtesy of John and Marilyn Yallop.*

This reamer is features some opalescence and transparency. *Courtesy of John and Marilyn Yallop.*

Less common orange reamers; none are marked. $80 each. *Courtesy of Randy Morey and Carol Miller.*

Less common lemon reamers; none are marked. $80 each. *Courtesy of Randy Morey and Carol Miller.*

Rare 7.5" (8" handle to handle) square, 3" deep refrigerator box with four tab handles. $125. *Courtesy of John and Marilyn Yallop.*

McKee Glass Company utilized more mold variations for jade-ite than for any other kitchen glassware. Left to right: 4" x 6" with a recessed knob (copied from Jeannette Glass Company), $175; 4" x 5" with raised ridges, $65; rare wedge, $250; 4" x 5", $45; on 5" x 8", $55. The two on the far right are the most common refrigerator box molds used by McKee. *Courtesy of Randy Morey and Carol Miller.*

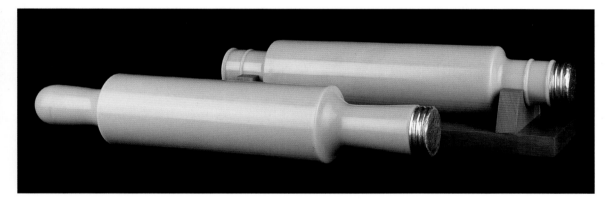

Rolling pins. Left/front: smooth handles, $300; right/back: ridged handles, $325. *Courtesy of Randy Morey and Carol Miller.*

Square shakers were offered in sets of two (salt and pepper) and sets of four, called range sets. Nutmeg was a later, additional shaker that is quite elusive. Pepper, $85; salt, flour, sugar, $120 each; nutmeg, $185. *Courtesy of Arnie Masoner.*

Rare embossed shakers, $400 each, with a 4" x 5" refrigerator box, $65. *Courtesy of Randy Morey and Carol Miller.*

Square shakers with large Deco lettering. Pepper, $100; salt, sugar, flour, $120; nutmeg, ginger, $140. *Courtesy of Arnie Masoner.*

Square shakers with small Deco lettering. Pepper, $100; salt, sugar, flour, $120; spice, $145. *Courtesy of Arnie Masoner.*

Roman Arch shakers with script lettering, $350 each. *Courtesy of Arnie Masoner.*

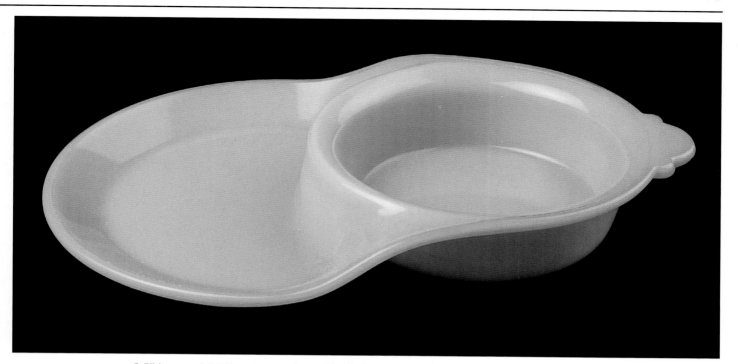

8.5" long and 6.25" across snack tray/child's feeding dish, $200.
Courtesy of Ken and Terri Farmer.

"Wash Stand Set." The tumbler is just over 5.5" tall. As shown, $300. Tumbler alone, $75.
Courtesy of Randy Morey and Carol Miller.

Three tumblers. Left: Just over 5.5" tall, $75; middle: 4.25" tall also used as an egg cup, $50; right: 3.75" tall juice-sized, $60. *Courtesy of Randy Morey and Carol Miller.*

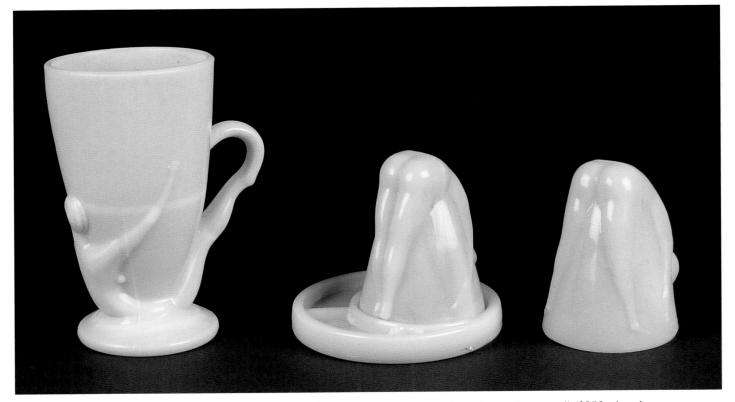

Left to right: Bottoms down mug (so named because the tushie is facing downward), $350; closed-legged bottoms up cocktail tumbler, $175; on a coaster, $100; and split-legged bottoms up cocktail tumbler, $275. McKee Glass Company originally manufactured the bottoms up tumblers with split legs. Look for patent number 77725 on legitimately old tumblers. *Courtesy of Todd Baum and Jesse Speicher.*

Water dispensers. Left: 4" tall with large rectangular lid, $300; right: 5" tall with small round lid, $200. *Courtesy of Randy Morey and Carol Miller.*

Sarah vases in four sizes. Left to right: 11" tall, $175; 6" tall, $100; 8" tall with horizontal ribs, $225; 8" tall, $175. The ribbed vase is the rarest. *Courtesy of John and Marilyn Yallop.*

Vase and candy jar. The dressed figure on the 8.5" triangle vase is more difficult to find than a nude one. When a lid is placed on the 7.5" tall vase it becomes a candy jar. These are found with a hole in the base for conversion to a table lamp. Left, $275; right base, $200; lid, $225. *Courtesy of Todd Baum and Jesse Spreicher.*

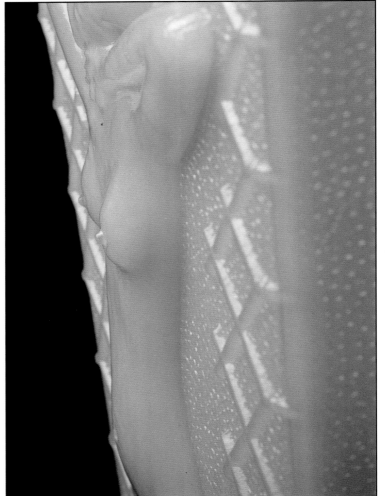

Detail of nude figure reveals the great detail of the design. *Courtesy of Denise Adams.*

Quality control was of little importance and as a result we are left with huge inconsistencies in color as shown by these three 8.5" tall No. 100 triangle vases. *Courtesy of Todd Baum and Jesse Spreicher.*

7.75" tall, 7.75" diameter "Modern Square" vase, $450. *Courtesy of Todd Baum and Jesse Spreicher.*

Pink Kitchen Glass

7.5" tall No. 100 triangle vase which is rarely seen in pink. *Courtesy of Todd Baum and Jesse Spreicher.*

3" tall creamer in the "Lenox" pattern introduced in 1930. *Courtesy of Randy Morey and Carol Miller.*

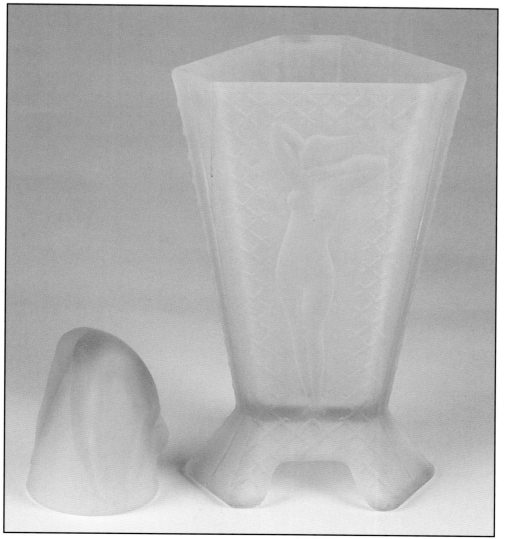

Satinized or frosted nude glassware is quite elusive. Shown is the 8.5" tall triangle vase that is actually drilled for conversion to a lamp and a 3.25" tall Bottoms up cocktail glass. Vase, $350; glass, $300. *Courtesy of Randy Morey and Carol Miller.*

Seville Kitchen Glass, Plain or Undecorated

Left: 9" diameter bowl that is part of a three bowl set. Not shown are the 7.5" diameter and 6" diameter bowls. From the early 1930s, this mold/shape is rarely seen as it was not used as frequently as the bell bowl molds. $100 each regardless of size. Right: 9" diameter, 4.5" deep bell bowl. $50 each regardless of size. *Courtesy of Randy Morey and Carol Miller.*

Left to right: 7" diameter a bowl with spout, $75; 6" diameter bell bowl, $50; tumbler or egg cup (used both ways), $40; measuring cup, $225. *Courtesy of Randy Morey and Carol Miller.*

Four bowls, left to right: 11.5", 9", 7.45+", 6", $45 each. *Courtesy of Randy Morey and Carol Miller.*

Three rimmed bowls. $45 each. *Courtesy of Clark Crawford.*

9.5" and 6" diameter rest-well styled bowls. The paneled details near the base of these bowls add to their value, as these are quite rare. A view from the underside shows how lovely this design is - a clear departure from the common bell bowl. $125 each. *Courtesy of Clark Crawford.*

40-ounce canisters. Plain canisters (without lettering) were designed to be refrigerator boxes. *Courtesy of Randy Morey and Carol Miller.*

Three 7.25" tall canisters with press-on lids. $225 each. *Courtesy of Randy Morey and Carol Miller.*

Five 7.5" tall square canisters with screw-on lids. $175 each. *Courtesy of Randy Morey and Carol Miller.*

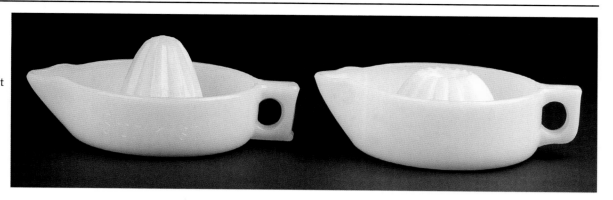

Left: orange reamer, $100; right: grapefruit reamer, $225. *Courtesy of Randy Morey and Carol Miller.*

7.5" (8" handle to handle) square, 3" deep refrigerator box with four tab handles. $125. *Courtesy of Todd Baum and Jesse Spreicher.*

Square shakers with large Deco lettering. Flour and sugar, $70 each; others, $85 each. *Courtesy of Todd Baum and Jesse Spreicher.*

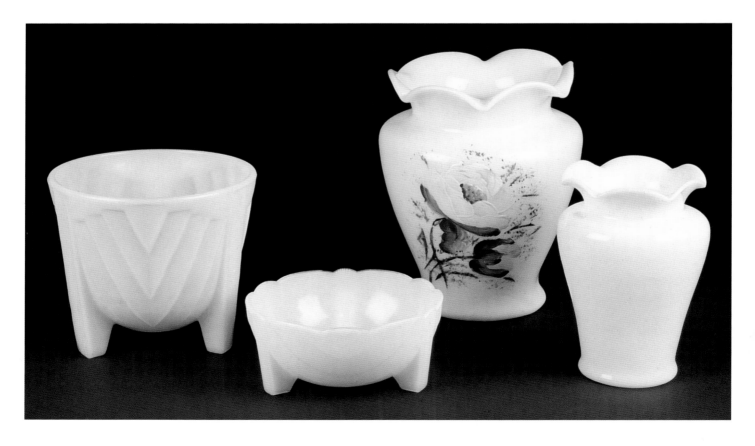

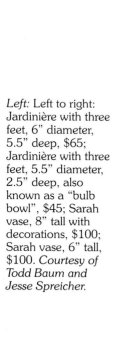

Left: Left to right: Square spice shaker, $35; three-part grill plate, $75; 4" x 5" refrigerator box, $50; 4" x 5" refrigerator box on 5" x 8" refrigerator box, $75. *Courtesy of Clark Crawford.*

Left: Left to right: Jardinière with three feet, 6" diameter, 5.5" deep, $65; Jardinière with three feet, 5.5" diameter, 2.5" deep, also known as a "bulb bowl", $45; Sarah vase, 8" tall with decorations, $100; Sarah vase, 6" tall, $100. *Courtesy of Todd Baum and Jesse Spreicher.*

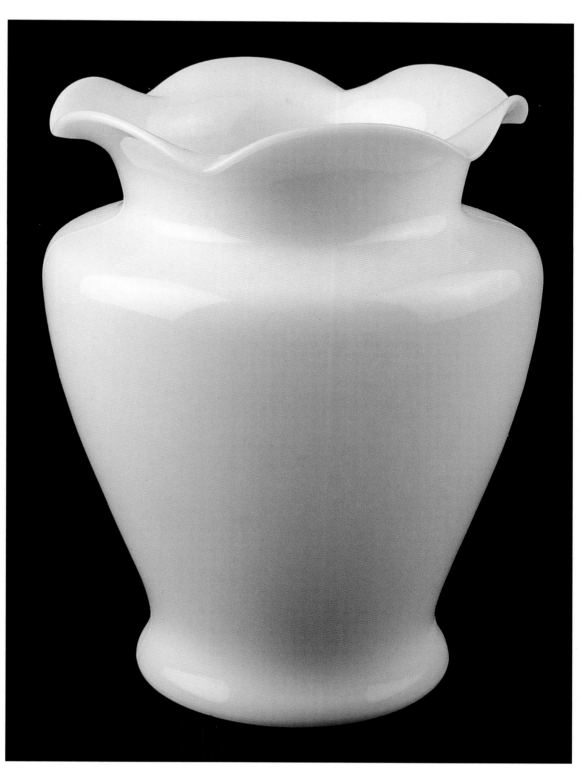

Sarah vase made in three sizes but shown in the 8" height. $100 each regardless of size. *Courtesy of John and Marilyn Yallop.*

Examples of nudes kitchen glass. Note: Look for the patent number 77725 on vintage nude tumblers and mugs. The triangle vase becomes a candy jar when it has a stacked lid as shown. Left to right: No. 100 triangle vase, 8" tall, $200; bottoms up cocktail glass, 3.25" tall, $175; bottoms down mug, 5.5" tall, $350; coaster for bottoms up cocktail glass, 4" diameter, $100; No. 100 triangle vase, 6" tall, $200; lid, $225. *Courtesy of Todd Baum and Jesse Spreicher.*

Seville Kitchen Glass with Decorations

9" diameter, 4.5" deep bell bowl with green dots. $175.
Courtesy of Tom Donlan.

9" diameter, 4.5" deep bell bowl with green trim and green stripe. $80.
Courtesy of Tom Donlan.

SEVILLE KITCHEN GLASS WITH BLACK GLASS

Left to right: 4" x 5" refrigerator box, 4" x 5" refrigerator box on 5" x 8" refrigerator box, 3.5" tall canister, 2.5" tall canister. $300 each. *Courtesy of Randy Morey and Carol Miller.*

WHITE KITCHEN GLASS, PLAIN OR UNDECORATED

9" bell bowl, $25; 7+" rimmed bowl with a pouring spout, $45; 4.25" egg beater bowl with a spout, $45. *Courtesy of Randy Morey and Carol Miller.*

5" x 8" refrigerator box, $35; 2.5" canister, $30; one-pound butter dish, $65. *Courtesy of Randy Morey and Carol Miller.*

Rare 5" tall canister , $150; 4.5" canister, $90; both labeled to hold sugar.
Courtesy of Randy Morey and Carol Miller.

5" tall canisters, a hard-to-find size. $125 each.
Courtesy of Randy Morey and Carol Miller.

4.5" tall canisters, the common size used again and again by McKee Glass Company. $90 each. *Courtesy of Randy Morey and Carol Miller.*

Canisters can also be found with white lids. The previous examples have clear lids. This 5" tall canister with the name in script was made in black as shown and red. $125. *Courtesy of Tom Donlan.*

Below: 4" x 5" drippings jar with 4" and 3.5" Roman Arch shakers. Drippings jar, $150; 4" shakers, $35; 3.5" shakers, $40. *Courtesy of Randy Morey and Carol Miller.*

Case of razor hones in store display box containing six 3" x 2.25" razor hones. $50 each as boxed, $20 each without box. *Courtesy of Randy Morey and Carol Miller.*

Coffee Hottles in the original package. Hottles were designed to hold hot beverages and liquids as they were made from heat-resistant glass, and were to be placed inside a coffee cup for stability as shown on the front of the brochure. Collectors show little interest in these but finding a complete boxed set is quite unusual. $50 as shown with box. *Courtesy of Randy Morey and Carol Miller.*

The smart - convenient way to serve coffee!

SAVES STEPS

Enjoy eating with your family and guests by using Hottles.

No need to interrupt your meal to serve seconds. Each person pours their coffee from the Hottle when desired.

For best results, place Hottle inside cup to keep coffee hot.

MADE OF HEAT RESISTANT GLASBAKE

The hottest beverages and soups may be poured into your Hottles without fear of breakage because they are made of famous heat-resisting Glasbake.

Your Hottles may be washed in modern dishwashers or in the dishpan without injury to either the plastic collar or the glass.

INDOOR-OUTDOOR

The attractively wrapped Hottle is a cheerful addition to the pleasure of bed tray service, in sickness and in health. The Hottle assures you of coffee in the cup and not in the saucer. Ideal for serving tea, soup or broth.

Your guests or family will love this most convenient and pleasant manner of serving hot beverages.

For the out of doors snack, you can serve without fear of cold coffee or the nuisance of going back and forth for refills.

COFFEE SERVED IN THE FINEST FASHION!

Two Hottles in the attractive display box are a gift that will be graciously received and more appreciated each time they are used.

PACKED

Each box contains two Hottles with plastic collars in contrasting colors.

Available at your local department stores.

McKEE GLASS COMPANY
JEANNETTE, PA.   •   U.S.A.
ESTABLISHED 1853

A variety of reamers, back row left to right: Sunkist with some opalescence, $225; Sunkist "Block" lettering in a box, $225; Valencia, $225. Front row left to right: Sunkist, $150; Valencia without a name, $150. *Courtesy of Arnie Masoner.*

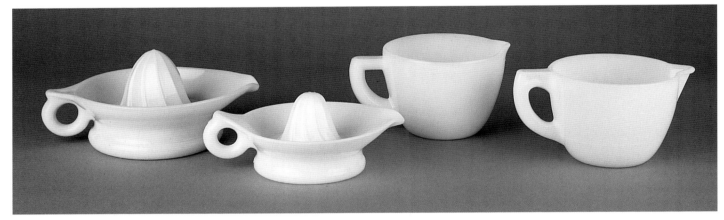

Left to right: orange reamer, lemon reamer, two-cup measures with different spouts. Reamers, $45 each; measures, $35 each. *Courtesy of Randy Morey and Carol Miller.*

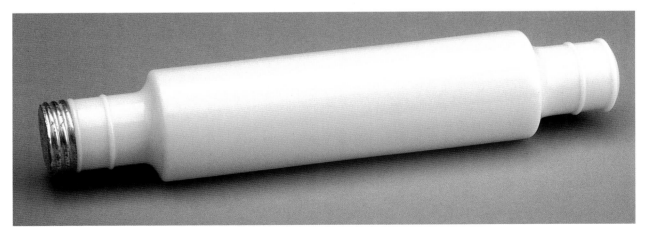

Rolling pin, $225. *Courtesy of Randy Morey and Carol Miller.*

Elusive 7.5" tea canister, $125; with 6" tall shakers, $80 each. *Courtesy of Randy Morey and Carol Miller.*

Deco embossed salt and pepper shakers, $45 each. *Courtesy of Randy Morey and Carol Miller.*

Square shakers with small and large Deco lettering, $55 each. *Courtesy of Randy Morey and Carol Miller.*

Square shakers. The Electrochef shakers are part of a four-piece range set that was probably free with the purchase of an Electrochef range, $70 each. Advertising shakers are more valuable than plain shakers and those with the circle around the labels are more valuable than the plain counterparts. Circles, $50 each; plain, $35 each. *Courtesy of Arnie Masoner.*

Vertically striped shakers are hard to find and whenever the names are thus written the value of the shaker immediately increases. $65 each. *Courtesy of Arnie Masoner.*

Roman Arch range set and canister. The sugar canister is the only canister produced with the Roman Arch design. Shakers, $35 each; canister, $300. *Courtesy of Arnie Masoner.*

A vintage decal decorates a sugar canister, $150. *Courtesy of Randy Morey and Carol Miller.*

Roman Arch range set with rare abstract design. Note the small "u" worked into an "S" to differentiate the sugar from the salt. $120 each. *Courtesy of Randy Morey and Carol Miller.*

3.75" tall Roman Arch shakers are prototypes with the original factory sticker on the bottom. These are too rare to price. *Courtesy of Todd Baum and Jesse Spreicher.*

This is the factory sticker on the side of the prototype shakers indicating "Shaker No. 37" and "Decoration No. 3." *Courtesy of Todd Baum and Jesse Spreicher.*

Roman Arch shakers with Bakelite lids and a matching drippings jar. Shakers, $35 each; drippings jar, $150. *Courtesy of Randy Morey and Carol Miller.*

4.25" tumbler/egg cup, $30; 7" diameter divided baby dish, $45; 3.75" tall flat tumbler. $35. *Courtesy of Randy Morey and Carol Miller.*

7.75" tall, 7.75" diameter "Modern Square" vase, $450.
Courtesy of Todd Baum and Jesse Spreicher.

White Kitchen Glass with Decorations

Abraham Lincoln

Roman Arch shakers, $125 each; one-pound butter dish, $250. *Courtesy of Randy Morey and Carol Miller.*

Advertisements

One-pound butter dish with advertisement, $150. *Courtesy of Randy Morey and Carol Miller.*

One-pound butter dishes with advertisements. $150 each. *Courtesy of Randy Morey and Carol Miller.*

Bowtie – Black

The black bowtie is extremely rare and these pieces are the only ones featured in this book. The drippings jar and the refrigerator box are obviously the same mold which are distinguished from one another by the addition of the black detailing. $300 each. *Courtesy of Randy Morey and Carol Miller.*

Bowtie – Red

6", 7", 8", 9" bell bowls, $125 each. *Courtesy of Randy Morey and Carol Miller.*

One-pound butter dish, $225; two-cup measure, $150; Roman Arch shakers, salt and pepper, $125 each; sugar and flour (available, but not shown), $175 each. Note the Bakelite lid on the sugar shaker. *Courtesy of Randy Morey and Carol Miller.*

Three drippings jars: 3.5" tall round with clear lid, $150; 2.5" tall with white lid, $125; 4" x 5" rectangle with white lid, $125. *Courtesy of Randy Morey and Carol Miller.*

4" x 5" refrigerator boxes on 5" x 8" refrigerator box all with clear lids and three canisters measuring 2.5" tall, 3.5" tall, and 4.5" tall all with white lids. $200 each. *Courtesy of Randy Morey and Carol Miller.*

Diamonds (Diamond Check)

Roman Arch shakers in three different colors. McKee Glass Company catalogues called this motif "Diamonds" but today's collectors and dealers identify this pattern as "Diamond Check." Shakers, $200 each. *Courtesy of Randy Morey and Carol Miller.*

Diamond in green is quite rare. Roman Arch shakers, 7" bell bowl, 5" x 8" refrigerator box. Not shown is the salt shaker, and one can assume 6", 8", and 9" bell bowls were manufactured as well as the 4" x 5" refrigerator box. $275 each. *Courtesy of Randy Morey and Carol Miller.*

Black Diamond 6", 7", 8" bell bowls and Roman Arch shakers. $200 each. *Courtesy of Randy Morey and Carol Miller.*

Red Diamond 2-cup measure and Roman Arch shakers in red and black. $200 each. *Courtesy of Randy Morey and Carol Miller.*

6", 7", 8", 9" bell bowls, $125 each. *Courtesy of Randy Morey and Carol Miller.*

One-pound butter
dish, $225. *Courtesy
of Randy Morey and
Carol Miller.*

The stacking canisters will store one inside the other and measure 2.5", 3.5", and 4.5"
tall. $125 each. *Courtesy of Randy Morey and Carol Miller.*

Roman Arch shakers, 4" x 5" refrigerator box on 5" x 8" refrigerator box. Shakers, $200
each; refrigerator boxes, $125 each. *Courtesy of Randy Morey and Carol Miller.*

Dots – Black and Red

Left to right: 9"+ mixer bowl, $175; Roman Arch shakers, $150 each; 8" bell bowl on 9" bell bowl, and 6" bell bowl; $150 each. The 7" bell bowl is not shown. *Courtesy of Randy Morey and Carol Miller.*

A 4.5" tall canister becomes a sugar canister when labeled. Obviously both of these canisters should have lids which would be plain, undecorated glass. With lids, sugar, $400; red, $300. *Courtesy of Arnie Masoner.*

Bell bowls with red dots. $125 each, $500 for the complete set of four. *Courtesy of Randy Morey and Carol Miller.*

Left to right: 9" + mixer bowl, $175; 7" and 9" bell bowls, $125 each. *Courtesy of Randy Morey and Carol Miller.*

Two-cup measure. $100. *Courtesy of Randy Morey and Carol Miller.*

6.25" tall square coffee canister with screw lid. $350. *Courtesy of Randy Morey and Carol Miller.*

Roman Arch shakers, two 4" x 5" refrigerator boxes and one 5" x 8" refrigerator box. $125 each. *Courtesy of Tom Donlan.*

Dots – Green

2.5" tall drippings jar, $350; four Roman Arch shakers, $200 each; and 9" bell bowl, $200. *Courtesy of Randy Morey and Carol Miller.*

Dots – Orange

4" Roman Arch shakers. $175 each. *Courtesy of Todd Baum and Jesse Spreicher.*

Flowers

Amaryllis blooms in bold bursts of red contrasting beautifully on pure white kitchen glass. This motif is quite elusive and all of these pieces are courtesy of Wilma Morey. We believe Wilma has all amaryllis kitchen glass McKee that has been made. *Courtesy of Wilma Morey.*

Five bell bowls measuring almost 10.5", 9", 8", 7", and 6". The largest bowl is a size McKee Glass Company rarely utilized. $85 each. *Courtesy of Wilma Morey.*

One-pound butter dish, $200; two-cup measure, $85. *Courtesy of Wilma Morey.*

Rectangular refrigerator boxes and round canisters, all with clear lids. The refrigerator boxes are 4" x 5" and 5" x 8". The stacking canisters will store one inside the other and measure 2.5", 3.5", and 4.5" tall. $85 each. *Courtesy of Wilma Morey.*

Miscellaneous Decoration

7", 8", and 9" bell bowls with rooster decorations. It is not known what else was made with this motif, but roosters have been a popular kitchen decorating theme for decades. $75 each. *Courtesy of Randy Morey and Carol Miller.*

4" x 5" refrigerator box with ivy decorations. It is not known what else was made with this motif that mimics a popular Hazel-Atlas design also of this era. $75. *Courtesy of Randy Morey and Carol Miller.*

Magic Chef salt and pepper shakers with red Bakelite lids. The "S" and "P" in the lids differentiate the two. $50 each. *Courtesy of Randy Morey and Carol Miller.*

Roman Arch shakers were produced with in a plethora of designs. The laurel wreath is hard to find and therefore more valuable than the shakers with the initials. Laurel wreath, $80 each; plain, $35. *Courtesy of Arnie Masoner.*

Pennsylvania Dutch Design

6", 7", 8", 9" and 10.25+" bell bowls. The largest bowl was not part of the original bowl sizes and helps to define newer designs like this one. The Pa. Dutch theme was a popular theme for kitchen décor; even Hoosier-type kitchen cabinets were decorated with this look that is not in favor with today's collectors which suppresses the value of these elusive pieces. $45 each. *Courtesy of Randy Morey and Carol Miller.*

Left to right: one-pound butter dish, $100; 2.5" tall and 4.5" tall canisters, $50 each; 4" x 5" refrigerator box on 5" x 8" refrigerator box, $50 each. *Courtesy of Randy Morey and Carol Miller.*

Ships – Black

Bowls left to right: 9+" mixer bowl, $90; 7" mixer bowl, $100; 7" and 9" bell bowls, $100 each. *Courtesy of Randy Morey and Carol Miller.*

Left to right: 2.5" tall drippings jar, $175; Roman Arch shakers, $150 each; 4" x 5" refrigerator box on 5" x 8" refrigerator box, $150 each. *Courtesy of Randy Morey and Carol Miller.*

Ships – Red

9", 8", 7", 6" bell bowls with red ships. $45 each, $180 for the complete set of four. *Courtesy of Randy Morey and Carol Miller.*

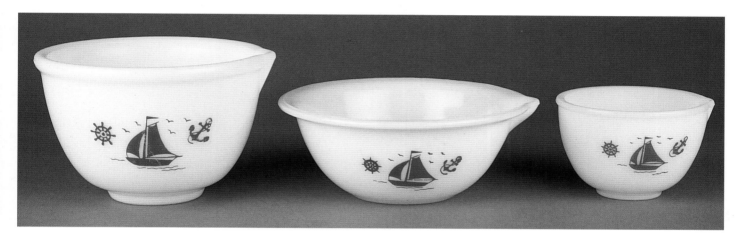

6.5" mixer bowl, $50; 7"+ bowl with a spout, $75; 4.25" egg beater bowl with a spout, $125. *Courtesy of Randy Morey and Carol Miller.*

9"+ mixer bowl, $50; 4" x 5" and 5" x 8" refrigerator boxes, $40 each. Note: The refrigerator boxes are found with clear and white lids. *Courtesy of Randy Morey and Carol Miller.*

2.5", 3.5", and 4.5" round canisters, $60 each; one-pound butter dish, $125; 4.25" tall tumbler or egg cup, $35. *Courtesy of Randy Morey and Carol Miller.*

Two 5.5" canisters: coffee and sugar. $150 each. *Courtesy of Randy Morey and Carol Miller.*

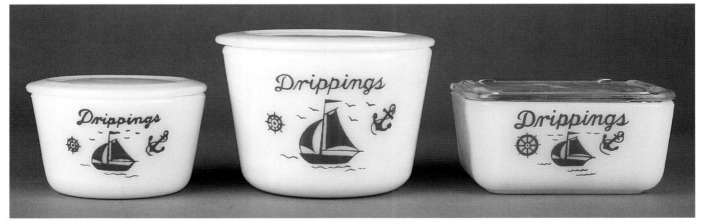

Three drippings jars: 2.5" round, 3.5" round, and 4" x 5" rectangle. Note: the round drippings jars are made from the same molds used to create the smallest round canisters, and the rectangular drippings jar is made from the same mold as the smaller refrigerator box. Left to right: $85, $150, $85. *Courtesy of Randy Morey and Carol Miller.*

This grouping shows how canisters were made with both clear and white lids. Also shown among the shakers and one-pound butter dish is another drippings jar with a plain base and Red Ships decorations on the lid. This unique drippings jar is worth $100. *Courtesy of Randy Morey and Carol Miller.*

Two-cup measures. The one on the left is a common mold, but the one on the right has a rarely-seen long spout. This odd measuring cup is marked "McK" and "Glasbake" making it a newer (but still old) design. Left, $85; right, $175. *Courtesy of Randy Morey and Carol Miller.*

Red Ships shakers were made in a variety of designs. Left to right: 4" tall Roman Arch shaker with original "stacked" lid, 3.75" tall Roman Arch shaker with original "stacked" lid, 3.75" tall Roman Arch shaker with original black Bakelite lid, square shaker with original red Bakelite lid. $40 each. *Courtesy of Randy Morey and Carol Miller.*

Shakers with Red Ship motif, $40 each. *Courtesy of Randy Morey and Carol Miller.*

Shakers with Red Ship motif, $40 each. *Courtesy of Randy Morey and Carol Miller.*

Strawberries

Pieces with this still-popular motif are extremely rare. Shown are the 8" and 9" bell bowls, $100 each; one-pound butter dish, $200. Not shown, two-cup measure, $125. One can assume the 6" and 7" bell bowls were made. *Courtesy of Randy Morey and Carol Miller.*

4" x 5" refrigerator box on 5" x 8" refrigerator box, $100 each; 2.5" tall, 3.5" tall, and 4.5" tall canisters, $100 each. *Courtesy of Randy Morey and Carol Miller.*

Trimmed

All four bell bowls shown with different colored rims: red, blue, green, yellow. Both Fire-King and Pyrex decorated bowls in these same colors now referred to as the "primary colors." $75 each. *Courtesy of Randy Morey and Carol Miller.*

6" and 7" bell bowls with red rims. $75 each. *Courtesy of Tom Donlan.*

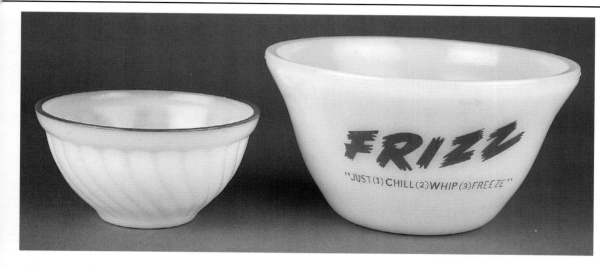

4.75" diameter swirled cracker bowl, $175; 7" bell bowl with advertisement, $60. *Courtesy of Randy Morey and Carol Miller.*

5" x 8" refrigerator box, $85; 8" bell bowl, $50; one-pound butter dish, $125. *Courtesy of Randy Morey and Carol Miller.*

Roman Arch shakers shown with and without trim. Plain, $35 each; trimmed, $50. *Courtesy of Randy Morey and Carol Miller.*

Pieces trimmed with a wide red band are not often seen. This comparison shows two applications of the red color. The red on the left rolls over the edge of the lid while the red on the right is a narrower band that reveals the white glass along the edge. *Courtesy of Randy Morey and Carol Miller.*

Canisters and refrigerator boxes are shown with wide red trim. The Roman Arch pepper shaker has a fine red line at the throat. Canisters and refrigerator boxes, $100 each; shaker, $50. *Courtesy of Randy Morey and Carol Miller.*

Part Two
Depression Glass Dinnerware

Close-up of pattern

McKee Glass Company is not considered an influential manufacturer of glass table settings when considering the vast quantities of glass created in conjunction with the Great Depression. This is rather ironic as McKee had evolved technologically more than most of their competition and was capable of mass producing glassware before other companies.

Laurel is one of two primary patterns created by McKee during this time period as it was produced in the 1930s. Laurel was produced in the opaque glass utilized in the manufacture of the kitchen glass pictured in this book. It is most often seen in French Ivory and Skokie Green isn't particularly difficult to find. Poudre Blue is rare but well worth the effort to find. Typically, one will find roughness around the edges and mold seams, as made. This dinnerware was mass produced with little or no concern for quality.

What follows is a listing of the pieces of glassware available in this pattern. The values are presented in dollars for items with scalloped edges; smooth, round edges reduce value by about 25%.

Skokie Green	**Other and Poudre**	**blue colors**
Bowl, 4.75" diameter, 1.75" deep berry	30	10
Bowl, 6" diameter 1.5" deep cereal	50	15
Bowl, 6" diameter, almost 2" deep with three feet	60	20
Bowl, 7.75" diameter soup	125	40
Bowl, 8.75" diameter 2.5" deep berry	100	30
Bowl, 9.75" oval vegetable	85	30
Bowl, 10.75" diameter with three feet	95	65
Bowl, 11" diameter	95	40
Candlestick, each	100	20
Cheese dish with lid	375	65
Base: 7.5" plate	25	25
Lid: 5" diameter	350	40
Creamer, 3"	45	15
Creamer, 4"	45	15
Cup	25	10
Plate, 5.75" sherbet	22	8
Plate, 7.5" salad plate/cheese dish base	25	25
Plate, 9" dinner	30	15
Plate, 9" grill	30	15
Platter, 10.75"	125	30
Salt and pepper shakers (pair)	300	75
Saucer	12	5
Sherbet, 3.75" diameter, 3.5" tall	30	12
Sugar, 3"	45	15
Sugar, 4"	45	15
Tumbler, 4.5" tall, 9 ounces	120	50
Tumbler, 5" tall, 12 ounces		90
Wine goblet/stem, 3.75" tall	185	75

French Ivory. Back row: 9" dinner plate, 9" grill plate; front row: cup and saucer, salt and pepper shakers, 3.5" tall sherbet on 5.75" sherbet plate. *Courtesy of Bill and Patti Foti.*

French Ivory. Back row: 8.75" diameter, 2.5" deep berry bowl; 6" diameter, 1.5" deep cereal bowl; front row: 6" diameter, almost 2" deep three-footed bowl; 4.75" diameter, 1.75" deep berry bowl. *Courtesy of Bill and Patti Foti.*

French Ivory. 3" and 4" creamers and sugars. *Courtesy of Bill and Patti Foti.*

French Ivory. Back row: 9" dinner plate, 4" creamer; front row: candlesticks; 4.75" diameter, 1.75" deep berry bowl, cup and saucer, shaker.

French Ivory. Cheese dish with lid. *Courtesy of Bill and Patti Foti.*

Skokie Green. Back row: 11" diameter bowl, 9.75" oval vegetable bowl; front row: 6" diameter, 1.5" deep cereal bowl, 4.75" diameter, 1.75" deep berry bowl. *Courtesy of Connie and Bill Hartzell.*

Skokie Green. 6" diameter, almost 2" deep three-footed bowl; shaker; 5.75" sherbet plate; 3" creamer; 3" sugar. *Courtesy of Connie and Bill Hartzell.*

Skokie Green. Back: 10.75" platter; front row: cheese dish with lid, candlestick, cup and saucer. *Courtesy of Connie and Bill Hartzell.*

Above: Skokie Green. 9" grill plate, 9" dinner plate, 9" dinner plate with smooth rim, 7.5" salad plate. *Courtesy of Connie and Bill Hartzell.*

Skokie Green. 3.75" tall wine goblet. *Courtesy of Staci and Jeff Shuck / Gray Goose Antiques.*

Poudre Blue. 11" diameter bowl; 9" dinner plate; 4.75" diameter, 1.75" deep berry bowl.
Courtesy of Todd Baum and Jesse Spreicher.

Poudre Blue. Back row: 10.75" platter, 9" dinner plate; front row: cup and saucer, 3"
creamer. *Courtesy of Vic and Jean Laermans.*

Poudre Blue. 8.75" diameter, 2.5" deep berry bowl.

Poudre Blue. 4" creamer. *Courtesy of Vic and Jean Laermans.*

Poudre Blue. 6" commemorative plate that reads, "FIFTY YEARS FORWARD, JEANNETTE, PENNSYLVANIA 1888-1938 JEANNETTE MCKEE CELEBRATION AUG. 28. SEPT. 5." *Courtesy of Samantha Parish.*

Only a few Depression Glass dinnerware patterns offer child's dishes, but Laurel is one of those patterns. A complete "Hostess Tea Set" consisted of one creamer and sugar and four cups, saucers, and 6" plates. These pieces were made plain in several colors, rimmed with color, and decorated with small black Scottish Terriers.

What follows is a listing of the pieces of glassware available in this pattern. The values are presented in dollars.

	Skokie Green	French Ivory	Decorated Rim	Scotty on Green	Scotty on Ivory
Creamer	35	50	150	120	65
Cup	30	40	125	75	50
Plate, 6"	20	25	125	75	30
Saucer	12	15	100	50	20
Sugar	35	50	150	120	65
Complete 14-piece set	318	370	1700	1040	530

"Hostess Tea Set" with a decorated rim. *Courtesy of Walt and Kim Lemiski / Waltz Time Antiques.*

"Hostess Tea Set" with a decorated rim and original box. *Courtesy of John and Cindy Frank.*

"Hostess Tea Set"
in "Skokie Green"
in an original box.
*Courtesy of John and
Cindy Frank.*

French Ivory cup
and saucer with
Scotty decora-
tions.

A view of the "Hostess Tea
Set box. *Courtesy of John
and Cindy Frank.*

ROCK CRYSTAL FLOWER DINNERWARE

Rock Crystal Flower is a heavy, well-made pattern reminiscent of 19th Century pressed glass. It is clear this dinnerware's roots are in early glassware which had been made for decades by McKee. Although McKee Glass Company's glassware from the Depression Era is notorious for being poorly finished, Rock Crystal Flower does not suffer from rough edges and sloppy mold seams. The glass is heavy enough to allow a measure of comfort to those uncomfortable with the concept of glass dishes.

This is a pattern with many options. There are thirteen bowls that range in size from a 4" diameter sauce bowl to a 12.5" diameter footed "center bowl" designed to be on display on a sideboard. Rock Crystal Flower has five goblets with the smallest having a capacity of four ounces and the largest having a capacity of eleven ounces. There are five Rock Crystal Flower pitchers:

1 Quart Squat, 5" tall, 3.75" inside diameter
½ Gallon Squat, s.e., 6.5" tall, 5" inside diameter
Fancy Tankard, 8.25" tall, 4.5" inside diameter
Covered Tankard, 9" tall, 4.25+" inside diameter
Fancy Tankard, 10.25" tall, 4.75" inside diameter

There is an assortment of eight plates, three relishes, and three trays offering a great deal of options for setting the table. There are even three vases for that added panache.

The palette of Rock Crystal Flower colors is almost staggering. As a pattern that was produced for a decade (1921-1931), McKee Glass Company had many opportunities to experiment with this pattern. Certainly some of the pieces that are now considered oddities were deliberate, but one must recognize that the creative efforts of factory workers with and without their supervisors' knowledge. An assortment of colors is presented here.

The original McKee Glass Company catalogue designated the two different edges found on this pattern with "s.e." for scalloped edge and "p.e." for plain edge, and this is used with the listing that follows:

ROCK CRYSTAL FLOWER	Red	Cobalt	Other Colors	Crystal	Qty
Bon bon, 7.5" s.e.	60	50	30	20	___
Bowl, 4" s.e., sauce	35	30	20	10	___
Bowl, 4.5" s.e., fruit	35	30	20	10	___
Bowl, 4.75" p.e.	65				___
Bowl, 5" s.e., fruit	45	35	25	15	___
Bowl, 5" p.e., finger	60	50	40	20	___
Bowl, 7" s.e., salad	65	55	35	25	___
Bowl, 8" s.e., salad	80	60	40	30	___
Bowl, 8.25" s.e.			160		___
Bowl, 8.5" p.e., open center handle	250				___
Bowl, 9" s.e., salad	120	100	50	25	___
Bowl, 10.5" s.e., salad	100	80	50	25	___
Bowl, 11.5" p.e., 5.75" tall w/foot			200		___
Bowl, 12.5" s.e., "Center Bowl", ftd.	300	450	150	75	___
Butter dish base				200	___
Butter dish lid				150	___
Butter complete				350	___
Cake stand, 11"	125	100	60	40	___
Candelabra, 2-lite, 5.25" tall, 6.5" wide, ea.	150	450	60	20	___
Candelabra, 3-lite, ea.	185	85	70	30	___
Candlestick, flat w/stem, ea.	70	60	40	20	___
Candlestick, 5.5", ea.	100	70	40	20	___
Candlestick, 8.5", ea.	225	175	80	40	___
Candy w/lid, 7" diam., 5" tall	250	200	80	60	___
Candy w/lid, 10.25" tall	275	225	100	70	___
Cheese & crackers	150		150		___
10.5" plate w/indent	75		75		___
3" tall, 4.25" diam. comport	75		75		___
Comport, 5.5" diam., 7" tall	100	80	50	40	___
Comport, 8.5" diam., 3.75" tall			85		___
Creamer, s.e., flat				30	___
Creamer, s.e., ftd., 4.25"	70	50	30	20	___
Cruet w/stopper, 6 oz.				100	___
Cup	70	50	20	15	___
Devilled egg plate				65	___
Goblet, 4 oz., 3.75"				15	___
Goblet, 7.5 oz, 5.75"	60	50	25	15	___
Goblet, 8 oz., 6.5"	60	50	25	15	___
Goblet, 8 oz., large footed	60	50	25	15	___
Goblet, 11 oz. iced tea	70	50	20	15	___
Ice Dish, 3 designs				35	___
Jelly, 5" s.e.	50	40	30	20	___
Lamp	750	600	350	225	___
Parfait, 3.5 oz.	80	60	40	20	___
Pitcher, 1 qt. squat, 5" tall, 3.75" inside diam.			250	175	___
Pitcher, ½ gal. squat, s.e. 6.5" tall, 5" inside diam.			200	130	___
Pitcher, Fancy Tankard, 8.25" tall, 4.5" inside diam.			200		___
Pitcher, Covered Tankard, 9" tall, 4.25+" inside diam.				300	___
Pitcher, Fancy Tankard, 10.25" tall, 4.75" inside diam.				200	___
Plate, 6" s.e., bread & butter	20	18	12	8	___
Plate, 7" p.e., under plate for finger bowl	20	18	12	8	___
Plate, 7.5" p.e. & s.e., salad	20	18	12	8	___
Plate, 8.5" p.e. & s.e., salad	30	20	18	10	___
Plate, 9" s.e., cake	65	45	25	20	___
Plate, 10.5" s.e., cake (small center design)	65	45	35	25	___
Plate, 10.5" s.e., dinner (large center design)	180	100	80	60	___
Plate, 11.5" s.e., cake	60	40	30	20	___
Punch bowl, 14", 2 styles				400	___
Punch bowl base, 2 styles				225	___
Relish, 11.5" p.e., 5-part				50	___
Relish, 11.5" p.e., 2-part		70	60	40	___
Relish, 14" p.e., 6-part			100	80	___
Relish, 7-part w/closed handles, p.e.				80	___
Salt & pepper			140	85	___
Salt dip				30	___
Sandwich server, center handle	150	100	60	40	___
Saucer	20	18	12	8	___
Sherbet/Egg, 3 oz.	70	50	30	15	___
Spooner				50	___
Stemmed 1 oz. cordial, 3"	70	50	50	25	___
Stemmed 2 oz. wine	60	40	30	20	___
Stemmed 3 oz. wine	60	40	30	20	___
Stemmed 3.5 oz. cocktail	50	30	25	20	___
Stemmed 6 oz. champagne/ tall sundae, 4.5"	40	30	25	20	___
Stemmed 7 oz. goblet, 5.75"	60	40	30	20	___
Stemmed 8 oz. goblet, 6.5"	60	40	30	20	___
Sugar base	50	40	30	20	___
Sugar lid	150	120	50	40	___
Sundae, 3.25", 6 oz., low foot	40	30	20	15	___
Syrup w/metal lid	800			200	___
Tray, 7" s.e., pickle or spoon				70	___
Tray, 12" s.e., celery	90	60	50	30	___
Tray, 13" p.e., roll	125	100	75	35	___
Tumbler, 2.5" whiskey	70	50	30	20	___
Tumbler, 5 oz. tomato juice, 3.5"	60	50	30	20	___
Tumbler, 4"	60	50	30	20	___
Tumbler, 5"	60				___
Tumbler, 5.25", 2 styles	60	50	30	20	___
Tumbler, 12 oz., 2 styles, iced tea	70	60	40	30	___
Vase, cornucopia			100	80	___
Vase, 7" tall, 5.5" diam.				65	___
Vase, 11" cupped	200	175	125	65	___
Vase, 12" w/square top	200	175	125	75	___

Note: Red slag 12.5" footed bowl, $450.

Courtesy of Lynn and Faye Strait.

Red. 6.5" goblet, 5.75" goblet, 3.25" sundae. *Courtesy of Ted Bradley.*

Red. 2.5" whiskey tumbler, 3.5" tomato juice tumbler, 4" tumbler, 5.25" tumbler. *Courtesy of Ted Bradley.*

Red is not red as shown by two stems made from the same mold but with a different mix of glass. *Courtesy of Chuck Mauric.*

Red. Creamer, sugar with lid, 4.75" diameter bowl, 9" covered tankard. *Courtesy of Ted Bradley.*

Red and red with variations. Back row: 8.5" salad plate, 7.5" salad plate; front row: 6.25" saucer with color variations, two cups with color variations; two cordials with color variations. *Courtesy of Chuck Mauric.*

Crystal. 3.5" cocktail, 11.5" two-part relish, 4.5" fruit bowl on 7" under plate for finger bowl.

Crystal. 13" roll tray. *Courtesy of Mike Rothenberger / Mike's Collectables.*

Crystal. Fancy tankard. *Courtesy of Bill Quillen.*

Crystal. 14" six-part relish. *Courtesy of Mike Rothenberger / Mike's Collectables.*

Crystal. One quart jug, 11" tall vase, 7" tall comport. *Courtesy of Faye and Robert Smith.*

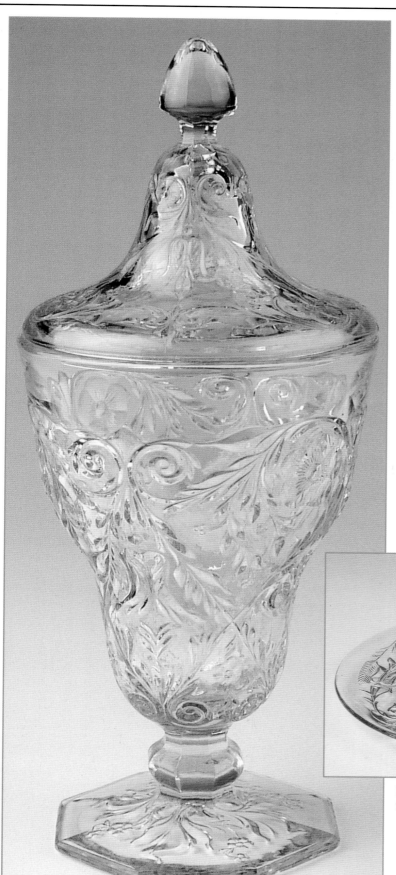

Pink. 10.25" tall candy jar with lid. *Courtesy of Roger LeBlanc and Bryce Mansell.*

Pink. Cheese and crackers: 10.5" base plate has an indent for the 3" tall comport. *Courtesy of Jewell Gowan.*

Amber. Back row: 10.25" tall candy jar with lid, 11" tall cupped vase; front row: 7" diameter, 5.5" tall low candy jar; 11.5" diameter, 5.75" tall footed bowl. *Courtesy of Mike and Leegh Wyse.*

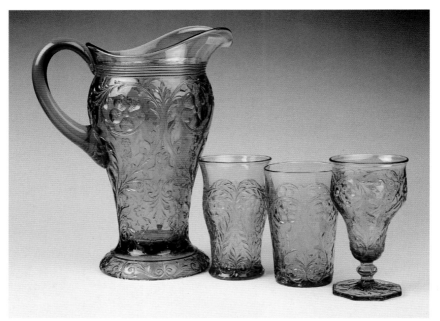

Amber. 8.25" tall fancy tankard, 5.25" tall tumblers in two style variations, 5.75" tall goblet. *Courtesy of Mike and Leegh Wyse.*

Amber. 10.75" diameter sandwich server with a center handle. *Courtesy of Larry Newton.*

Green. One quart squat jug, 11.5" diameter cake plate, 3.25" tall sundae on 6" bread and butter plate. *Courtesy of Mike and Leegh Wyse.*

Green. 2.25" tall candlestick. *Courtesy of Joanne Aldrich.*

Green. 5.75" tall gob-
let. *Courtesy of Mike
and Leegh Wyse.*

Multiple colors. 4.5" diameter, 1.5" deep fruit bowls in amethyst, green, ice blue, and crystal with gold trim. *Courtesy of Joanne Aldrich.*

Green, but a slightly different shade. 12.5" diameter "Center Bowl."
Courtesy of Stephen Spaid.

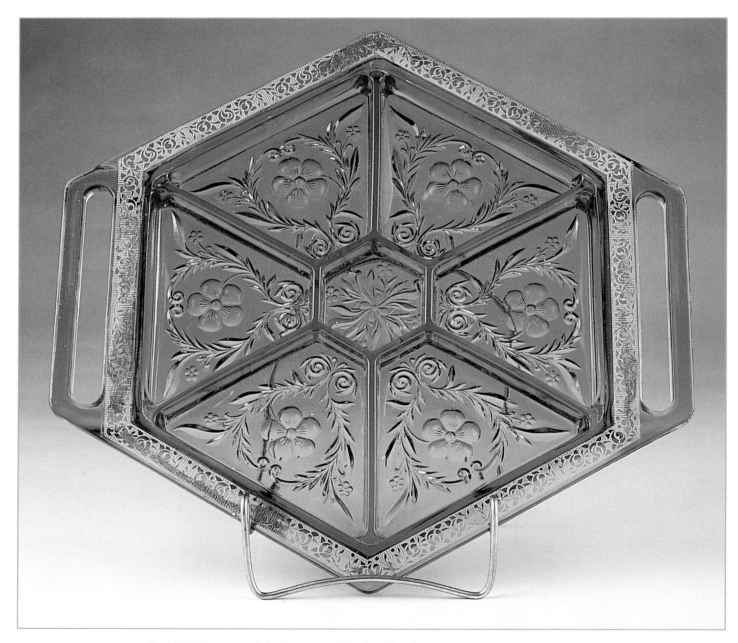

Teal. 14" diameter relish. *Courtesy of Stephen Spaid.*

Ice Blue. 10.25" diameter, 3.5" deep bowl. *Courtesy of Rick Hirte / Sparkle Plenty Glassware.*

Vaseline. 10.25" diameter, 3.5" deep bowl. *Courtesy of Jewell Gowan.*

Bibliography

http://antiques.about.com
http://glassandpotterysellers.org
http://henonnest.com
http://homepages.rootsweb.com
http://reviews.ebay.com
http://us.history.wisc.edu
http://www.carnivalheaven.com
http://www.decades.com
http://www.earlyamericanworkshop.com
http://www.glassian.org
http://www.myinsulators.com
Weatherman, Hazel Marie. *Colored Glassware of the Depression Era 2.* Oazark, MO: Glassbooks, 1978.

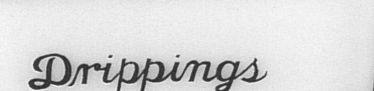

Index

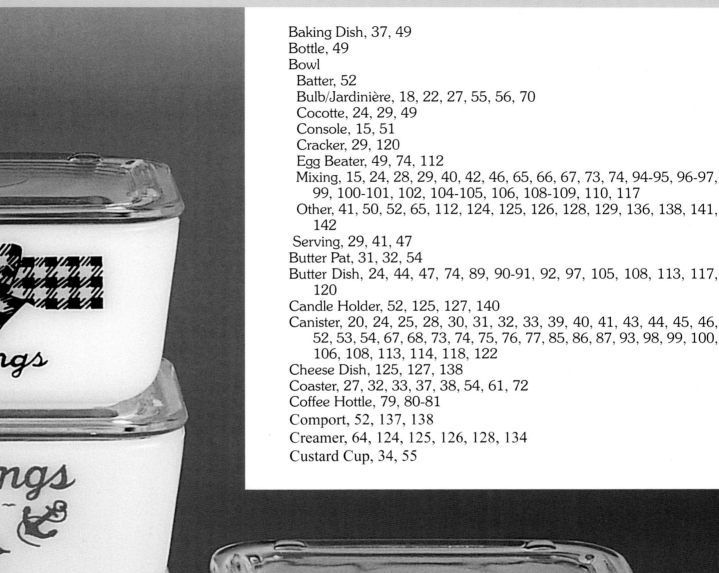

Baking Dish, 37, 49

Bottle, 49

Bowl
  Batter, 52
  Bulb/Jardinière, 18, 22, 27, 55, 56, 70
  Cocotte, 24, 29, 49
  Console, 15, 51
  Cracker, 29, 120
  Egg Beater, 49, 74, 112
  Mixing, 15, 24, 28, 29, 40, 42, 46, 65, 66, 67, 73, 74, 94-95, 96-97,
     99, 100-101, 102, 104-105, 106, 108-109, 110, 117
  Other, 41, 50, 52, 65, 112, 124, 125, 126, 128, 129, 136, 138, 141,
     142
  Serving, 29, 41, 47

Butter Pat, 31, 32, 54

Butter Dish, 24, 44, 47, 74, 89, 90-91, 92, 97, 105, 108, 113, 117,
     120

Candle Holder, 52, 125, 127, 140

Canister, 20, 24, 25, 28, 30, 31, 32, 33, 39, 40, 41, 43, 44, 45, 46,
     52, 53, 54, 67, 68, 73, 74, 75, 76, 77, 85, 86, 87, 93, 98, 99, 100,
     106, 108, 113, 114, 118, 122

Cheese Dish, 125, 127, 138

Coaster, 27, 32, 33, 37, 38, 54, 61, 72

Coffee Hottle, 79, 80-81

Comport, 52, 137, 138

Creamer, 64, 124, 125, 126, 128, 134

Custard Cup, 34, 55

Decanter, 49
Dinnerware, 123-142
Egg Cup, 21, 61, 65, 88, 113
Goblet, 56, 127, 133, 139, 140
Hostess Tea Set, 130-132
Lighter, 38
Measuring Cup, 47, 65, 83, 92, 96, 98, 101, 105, 115, 117
Mug, 61, 72
Jar
  Candy, 18, 52, 63, 72, 137, 138
  Cookie, 18, 56

  Drippings, 33, 43, 44, 45, 46, 76-77, 88, 91,
    92, 102, 110-111, 114
  Sterilizer, 17, 37
Razor Hone, 15, 17, 24, 78
Reamer
  Other, 21, 34, 56-57, 69, 82, 83
  Sunkist, 15, 21, 34, 56, 57, 69, 82
Refrigerator Box, 33, 35, 39, 40, 41, 42,
    43, 44, 45, 47, 52, 57, 58, 59, 68, 69,
    71, 73, 74, 91, 93, 94, 98, 102-103,
    106, 107, 108, 110-111, 112, 114,
    118, 120, 122
Rolling Pin, 34, 58, 82-83
Salt Box, 29
Saucer, 20, 123, 125, 127, 128, 130, 135
Shakers
  Roman Arch, 16-17, 19, 24, 25, 28, 35, 39,
    40, 41, 42, 44, 45, 47, 60, 76-77, 86, 87,
    88, 89, 92, 94-95, 96, 98, 99, 102-103, 107,
    110-111, 115, 121, 122
  Square, 16, 20, 25, 35, 36, 58, 59, 70, 71, 84, 86,
    115
Tray
  Other, 37, 136
  Snack tray/child's feeding dish, 37, 60
Tumbler
Bottoms up, 15, 27, 64, 72
Other, 17, 21, 24, 33, 60, 61, 65, 88-89, 113, 134, 139
Vase
  Modern Square, 22, 63, 89
  Other, 138, 138
  Sarah, 18, 21, 38, 62, 70-71
  Triangle/nude, 18, 22, 23, 26, 38, 48, 62-63, 64, 72
Wash Stand Set, 60
Water Dispenser, 38, 61
Window Box, 19

CEREAL TEA COFFEE FLOUR

SALT PEPPER FLOUR SUGAR

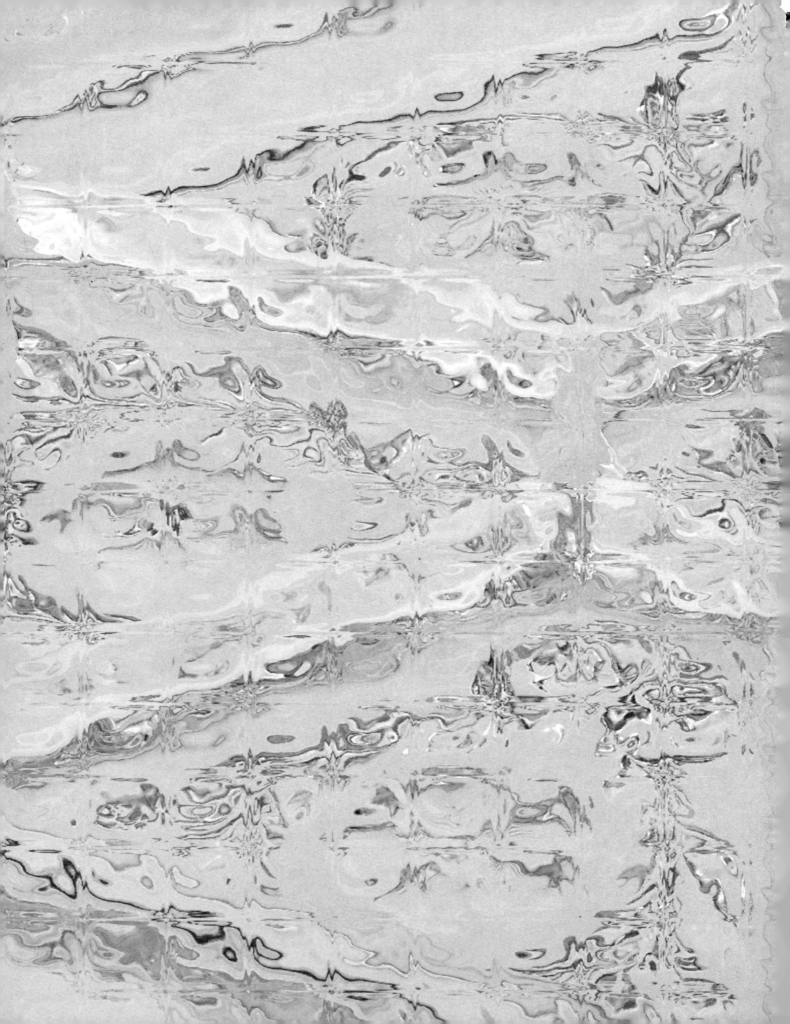